Fran—
Happy Memories to my
former French tutor

Tim

Christmas '91

TRADITIONAL HOUSES OF
RURAL FRANCE

TRADITIONAL HOUSES OF
RURAL FRANCE

BILL LAWS

PHOTOGRAPHY BY
JOHN FERRO SIMS

COLLINS & BROWN

JACKET ILLUSTRATIONS: FRONT
*Saint Germain-la-Campagne,
Normandy;* BACK LEFT *Lacoste,
Provence;* BACK RIGHT *Avallon,
Burgundy.*

First published in Great Britain in 1991
by Collins & Brown Limited
Mercury House
195 Knightsbridge
London SW7 1RE

Copyright © Collins & Brown 1991

Text copyright © Bill Laws 1991

Photographs copyright © John Ferro Sims 1991

The right of Bill Laws to be identified as the author of
this work has been asserted by him in accordance with
the Copyright, Designs and Patents Act 1988

A CIP catalogue record for this book
is available from the British Library

ISBN 1 85585 021 4

Conceived, edited and designed by Collins & Brown

EDITORIAL DIRECTOR: Gabrielle Townsend
EDITOR: Jennifer Chilvers
ART DIRECTOR: Roger Bristow
DESIGNED BY: Gill Della Casa

Filmset by Servis Filmsetting Limited, Manchester
Reproduction by J. Film, Thailand
Printed and bound in Hong Kong

FRONTISPIECE: JOUCAS, PROVENCE
*A large limestone house with a roof
of Roman tiles.*

CONTENTS

INTRODUCTION 6
SHADES OF DIFFERENCE 8 • NORMANDY 28 • BRITTANY 50
BURGUNDY 68 • PROVENCE 88 • DORDOGNE 112 • PAYS BASQUE 134
GLOSSARY 158 • INDEX 158 • ACKNOWLEDGEMENTS 160

INTRODUCTION

LEFT: LOCAL DISTINCTIVENESS
The traditional buildings of rural France reflect regional identity. Neither pretentious in style nor coarse in character, they were built by people with a deep understanding of natural materials and a sympathetic sense of design.

'All shades of difference are fast vanishing now in France. In fifty years' time there will be no Provençals left, and no Provençal language,' predicted the French writer Stendhal in 1838.

He was wrong. A hundred and fifty years later, the 'shades of difference' still survive in rural France. An industrial revolution, two world wars and unparalleled social upheaval have failed to crush the regional spirit.

France is like a pyramid, the whole supported by a mass of individual and sometimes fiercely independent parts. On the top stone stands the symbol of a united nation, Marianne for *La République*, wrapped in the *tricolore* and lustily singing the 'Marseillaise'. Perhaps Monsieur Bibendum the Michelin man is up there with her, a rakish beret on his head and a glass of champagne in his fat-fingered hand. But supporting them is the plurality and the diversity of this rural nation, a country composed of twenty-two regions, ninety-six departments, and 30,000 villages, each with its own personality.

Rural France presents the traveller with a mosaic of quiet country landscapes and distinctive building styles. Each encounter may not be an uplifting experience. French planning laws or the lack of them have permitted ribbon development, urban sprawl and some hideous buildings in which the architects responsible deserve to be incarcerated. The buildings which do please the eye and grace the countryside were put up without architectural assistance. Made to local designs in local materials and by local people, these rural buildings manage to maintain the physical presence of Stendhal's 'shades of difference'.

The French coined the term *vive la différence* and then incorporated it into the fabric of their homes. You do not need a degree in architecture to distinguish between the mellowed barns of Normandy and the moonlit limestone of a Dordogne farmhouse, between the cool, black slate of a Breton fishing cottage and the glazed tiles of a Burgundy roof. The fascination of France lies in the discovery of its local buildings, the humble architecture that is the true face of France.

SHADES OF DIFFERENCE

ONCE UPON A TIME, so long ago no one will ever know, somebody built the first house. Perhaps it was near Périgueux, that cultural centre of prehistoric France. *Homo sapiens* has occupied the tortured, limestone landscape around the Vézère and Dordogne rivers for 40,000 years and it is easy to imagine one of the anonymous Stone Age artists, responsible for the paintings at Lascaux, becoming increasingly unhappy with his damp and draughty cave. He is an intelligent man and he reasons that if he constructed a shelter close to the water supply, with its front to the dawn and its back to the westerly winds, life would be altogether more agreeable.

Being between commissions and having spare time on his hands, he builds a rectangular, low, stone wall, sets two posts and a ridge pole within the walls and covers the roof with a hurdle of woven saplings. His attempts at thatching are a dismal failure and he resorts instead to roofing with thin limestone slabs, dredged from the river. He forms a small hole at one end to vent the fire smoke.

The painter's brothers call by and gruntingly admire his handiwork. The womenfolk are even more impressed and nag their partners to make a similar dwelling for their own families: gradually a village of Dordogne stone is born.

It is a fanciful theory but based on the reality that rural people traditionally built their homes along these lines. Practical designs evolved, founded on function rather than fashion. Subject to changing climate and influenced by the odd conquest or colonization, the appearance of these buildings continued to be conditioned by the use of local materials, the earth, stone and wood of the neighbourhood.

Primitive designs evolved slowly, but 5,000 years ago country people in the western Celtic fringes had already constructed houses which would survive right down to our moon-conquering present. And by the Middle Ages, Mediterranean, Alpine, forest, moorland and hill people had each come up with a functional and distinctive solution to their housing problem.

These were men of pith and thew,
Whom the city never called;
Scarce could read or hold a quill,
Built the barn, the forge, the mill.

EDMUND BLUNDEN,
'FOREFATHERS'

LEFT: PURPOSEFUL POSITION
There was nothing random about the siting of traditional buildings. This Provençal farm, for example, stretched out along a rich valley in the Vaucluse, was deliberately placed with its front to the sun and its back to the worst of the weather.

The low, stone and thatched cottages of the Atlantic coast, the whitewashed rubble and red tiled roofs of the Mediterranean, the timber-framed houses of the hardwood forests, the moorland mud huts and the balconied chalets of the mountains—every mountain, as they say in the Jura, has its own distinctive building.

These country farms and cottages, pig sheds and byres, barns and dovecots which seemed to the English poet Wordsworth to 'rise by an instinct of their own, out of the native rock' have become a natural feature of the rural landscape. The humble highland and lowland homes of rural France would still be recognizable to a medieval time traveller who slipped into the twentieth century, and he might even be able to locate his landing position from surrounding vernacular styles such as the multi-gabled, timbered houses of Alsace or the earth-walled and thatched cottages of the Vendée.

The vernacular tradition (vernacular means literally a slave born in his master's house and therefore a native) provides a serviceable

ABOVE: HUMBLE HOMES
Much attention has been focused on the ecclesiastic, civic and grand domestic architecture of France. Little has been written about more modest buildings like these riverside houses in Oloron-Sainte-Marie in south-west France.

LEFT: BURGUNDY STREET SCENE
The vernacular tradition covers those buildings which were built, often by the occupants themselves, from local materials. The design varied from region to region, even from parish to parish, and gave each place its own distinctive look.

RIGHT: FORM AND FUNCTION
Climate and geography shaped the original character of folk architecture with mountain, marshland, forest and lowland environments each dictating its own design. This farmhouse in the Pyrenees housed the stock on the ground floor and the family above.

LEFT: SOCIAL CHANGE
Resistant to change for change's sake, craftspeople used the same techniques for centuries. The results, seen here in a Burgundy village, expressed regional personality. While in the sixteenth century the artisans brought their skills to bear on more imposing buildings, by the late nineteenth century their work was confined to smaller, less pretentious buildings.

definition of these domestic and agricultural buildings, designed to deal with the worst of the weather, built with materials that lay close to hand, or more usually underfoot, and which departed as little from the neighbour's building as possible.

Rural people are both inherently conservative and frugally opportunistic. If a local style evolved which used, for example, a half-hipped roof, then that roof was repeated again and again. If a more suitable and less expensive roofing material appeared, the builder promptly adopted it but forced it to conform to the traditional design. When slate replaced straw on the swept dormer roofs of the Breton cottage, the slate was cut like a thatch over the dormer; when the Basques learned to cut and shape their granite, they used it in place of oak in the *maison labourd* but held fast to the original design.

Why such resistance to new ideas? Stendhal gives a clue to this rural conservatism in a passage from *Le Rouge et le Noir*:

> To win public esteem in Verrières, it is essential, while building walls, not to adopt any sort of plan imported from Italy by the stonemasons passing every spring through the Jura gorges on their way to Paris. Such an innovation would brand the builder of walls for ever as a rebel against accepted convention, and damn him without redemption in the eyes of those prudent and sagacious persons who assess a man's reputation in Franche-Comté.

The country builder's intransigence is but one of the factors responsible for the rich inheritance of weathered buildings that gives rural France its captivating and timeless quality. Despite the big towns and cities, the industrial zones and the worst of the tourist development, France has kept faith with much of its rural landscape and many of its distinctive regional buildings.

City people often make two arrogant assumptions about their country cousins. The first is that they are, if not half-witted, then certainly slow-witted. The second is that they live their lives in a pastoral paradise. The metropolitan mind fails to appreciate that if the latter were true, the former must be false—if country people are so dull, how did they manage to find nirvana?

The urban French, who are at least a generation closer to their peasant past than most western Europeans, do not so easily confuse rural with rustic. Their rural roots are sometimes evident in a sepia portrait of the grandparents, hung with veneration in the suburban apartment. Grandfather, forcing a gap-toothed smile despite the discomfort of his hired suit, stands beside his stiff seated wife, hair professionally coiffured for the occasion, but still looking like craggy mutton dressed as lamb with her sun-blown features and milking hands, gnarled as tree roots, folded in her lap. City people like to keep close contact with such a recent past: the second home, the *résidence secondaire*, is not the prerogative of the wealthy and there is a detectable surge in village populations during weekends and holidays.

Another historical factor which played its part in the preservation of French folk architecture is fashion. Like anything else, rural architecture will alter if the inhabitants find it embarrassingly unfashionable and can afford to do something about it. To say the French are aware of fashion is to understate the case: they are not only driven by it, they create it. And for 600 years French fashion has

RIGHT: TRACES OF THE PAST
A classical arch is overlaid with coursed stonework in a Provençal wall. The whole of France was colonized at some stage in its history and foreign methods and materials, like the Roman roofing tiles of the Mediterranean, were often adopted by local builders.

RIGHT: FASHIONABLE FAÇADE
Fashion influenced the vernacular traditions. This shopfront, imposed on the face of a plain stone house in Provence, manages not to look out of place, but insensitive improvements can destroy the character of indigenous architecture.

emanated from one region, the Île-de-France, and one city, Paris. The Île-de-France began to concentrate political, social and cultural life around itself from the twelfth century onwards, eclipsing formerly powerful regions like Burgundy, and allowing Paris to dictate national style and dominate architectural expression.

In the Middle Ages the towns of the Paris basin were heavily fortified: building room was limited by the confines of the city walls and houses were squeezed upwards to maximize the restricted space. The descriptive french window, a universal building term for a tall

LEFT: CHANGING FACE
The earliest buildings relied upon the most basic materials: earth, stone and timber. When new materials, like brick or clay tiles, became available, they would be manufactured locally and used to replace the old. Here a thatched roof has been exchanged for a roof of clay tiles. The advent of cheap, mass-produced building materials eventually brought the vernacular period to an end.

LEFT: NEW TECHNOLOGY
The traditional buildings of the Basque country are among the most distinctive in France and early buildings, like this one at Ainhoa, were constructed in wood. When masonry tools, capable of dressing the local granite, became more widely available, the Basques retained the central timber frame but extended the house in stone.

window two or three times as high as it is wide, was only the result of so much urban verticality, similarly expressed in the roofs and defensive walls. When these city walls came down, to be replaced by boulevards and ring roads, the rest of France duly copied their example and established a pattern of town planning that is envied world-wide.

Moreover, the provinces doggedly toed the Paris line with their civic buildings when the French Renaissance style, a synthesis of the classical and the traditional, blossomed and flowered under the patronage of Louis XIV. When the royal court insisted on keeping tree-lined, equestrian highways radiating out from the city centre to the royal hunting grounds, the idea not only influenced the rest of France but, as with the Mall in Washington DC, travelled as far afield as the New World.

If the French king, that wealthy arbiter of refined taste had, like the Romanian despot Ceausescu, insisted that vernacular architecture was *passé*, poverty alone would have prevented the traditional rural rootstock from being dug up and destroyed. But a curious thing was happening at court: while Louis XVI was enduring the fawning admiration of his courtiers over the splendour of Versailles, his wife Marie Antoinette was playing at milkmaids at Le Hameau, the pseudo-rustic hamlet in the grounds of Le Petit Trianon at Versailles.

It must have raised a wry smile on the sunburnt faces of the provincial peasant, rubbing goose fat into her chapped hands as she hauled the milking stool out of the barn at five o'clock in the morning. But the implications were not lost on her fashion-conscious feudal landlord and his lady. Rural was not only acceptable: it had been awarded the royal seal of approval. The French never forgot, and a combination of fashionable pride and rural conservatism led to the vernacular style being preserved long after the royal heads had rolled.

France had a third good reason for maintaining its regional style. Extreme centralization provoked an equally extreme regional reaction, and reluctant people like the Bretons or the Basques developed a partisan attitude to central government interference. In these regions the indigenous architecture exhibited a proud indifference to the state style and rigidly adhered to its own.

Recognizing regional styles, the Alpine chalet, the Provençal *cabanon*, the Norman longhouse or the Basque *Labourd*, is not difficult. But Stendhal's shades of difference go deeper than regional boundaries. As every city has its quarters—Montmartre, Montparnasse, Saint-Germain-des-Prés in Paris for example—so every rural region has its distinctive districts, its *pays*. Thirty *pays* are stitched together to form Champagne, thirty-seven in Gascony, twenty-five at least in Burgundy and each *pays*, historically and geographically distinct from its neighbours, reflects the local topography. Creeping urbanization and the modern road network tend to erode the old boundaries, and

RIGHT: FITTING INTO THE LANDSCAPE
The siting of a settlement depended upon local topography. Surrounded by its crops, compact villages, like Vougeot on the rich plains of Burgundy, took up as little of the fertile land as possible.

LEFT: SAFE FROM INVASION

The inhabitants of Vaison-la-Romaine had one eye on defence and the other on the availability of a secure water supply when they established their Provençal hill village. The terrain would later protect it from the worst invasion of the twentieth century – traffic.

RIGHT: RIVER TRAFFIC

Less affluent than their Burgundian counterparts, rural communities like La Roque-Gageac tucked themselves in between limestone cliffs and the Dordogne river so as to profit from passing river trade.

BELOW: MOUNTAIN PASS

The high Pyrenees were neither generous nor fertile places. Too many neighbours meant too many people chasing a limited supply of food. As a consequence, mountain hamlets were isolated and scattered.

yet the identity of each *pays* survives in the faces of its folk architecture, not least because people built their farms, barns and cottages with whatever the local geology had to offer.

A geological map of France looks as if its maker abandoned cartography for art's sake and used the marbling technique of ink in water to create intricate patterns on the paper. Slates and shales, chalks and clays, limestones and sandstones, marbles and granites flow across the map as they meet and mingle beneath the French soil. Even where the same rock formation outcrops among a group of villages, no two quarries will produce identical stone and the appearance of the vernacular buildings reflects the changes.

Take Normandy where one village raised its houses in knapped flint and handmade bricks, while ten kilometres away the flint gives way to oak-framed houses, the timbers infilled with brick in a herringbone pattern. Another ten kilometres away, the brick clay is no longer available and wattle and daub predominates. Still further on, there is a hamlet where, because a pliable limestone turned up in the local quarry, cottages and barns have that mellowed stone look of a Dordogne village.

In Brittany the builder had to work the intractable granite, but give him a bit of malleable sandstone and the single-storey Breton cottage promptly disappears. In the Landes de Lanvaux one hill range is formed from a strikingly beautiful purplish stone and the vernacular buildings glow in this unlikely colour.

For centuries vernacular buildings served to house the people and their rural industries, and two hundred years after the revolution the old designs survive in some curious modern imitations: telephone cabins in the Dordogne take a Périgourdin roof; miniature replicas of the thatched and whitewashed Camargue *cabane* are built as tourist gites; a gargantuan petrol station mimics the shape of the traditional *Labourd* in the Pays Basque; and toy-sized timber-framed houses serve as bird boxes in Normandy gardens.

Across the Channel, their British neighbours also capitalized on their own vernacular styles, but insisted on shuffling designs around from one part of the country to another. Thus one can buy a modern Wealden house, originally a native of Kent, in the depths of Celtic

BELOW: DECORATIVE DETAIL
Ornamentation on traditional buildings was simple and minimalistic. Decoration tended to be reserved for the central feature of the house, the doorway. The carved lintel above this Pyrenean door is complemented by the supporting stones projected in beyond the door line.

RIGHT: PRIMITIVE AND POLITE
The vernacular tradition, which sits somewhere between primitive and polite architecture, was no less graceful than architect-designed buildings, expressed in this exposed inner wall at Avallon.

Wales or a western Purbeck house in eastern England. The result is a pastiche and a sad loss of local identity.

Imitating traditional styles is laudable enough and can be a great improvement on much modern architecture provided it echoes the local style and is not exported to water down the identity of another district. Folk architecture, like certain wines, does not travel well. In any case, the vernacular tradition is finished. It died when the neighbourhood quarry closed, the village brickworks went out of business and the local saw pit was filled in and grassed over. It died from natural causes, a death as inevitable as that which caused the demise of the primitive earth hut or the limestone cave. Local materials could not compete with the cheap building materials of the industrial age, the factory-made brick, the machine-made tile, the concrete lintel and softwood window frames. As their use died out, the skills of local craftspeople died with them.

France has inherited a rural rootstock of traditional buildings, each of which tells a story about the past. As time goes on, these stories are quietly slipping away. Over the next century, many of the buildings in this book will be pulled down to make way for a new housing estate, a motorway or, the current blight on the landscape, a hypermarket. A few will simply fall down, never to be rebuilt, while others will be improved beyond recognition. The insensitive restoration of each forge, granary, cottage, mill or farmhouse is like removing an old master from the Louvre, scrubbing the canvas clean and rehanging the picture with a factory-produced print in the original frame. Too many old buildings have been lost in this way.

When people take to the tourist trail in search of scenic beauty, they tend to judge a place's claim to fame by the quality of its landscape rather than by the beauty of its indigenous buildings. Information centres prod them in the direction of panoramic views or ancient ruins, anything in short which fuels their fascination for the spectacular. In the following chapters an attempt has been made to redress the balance by looking at six rural regions of France and in particular at some of the regional architecture which rarely gets a mention in the tourist guide but which makes these landscapes what they are: local, distinctive and worth conserving.

BELOW: AGRICULTURAL REVOLUTION
The twentieth century has seen the French farmer moving rapidly away from a peasant-based, agricultural economy. As a result, traditional buildings, like this barn in the Pyrenees, will become redundant unless alternative uses are found for them.

RIGHT: UNCERTAIN FUTURE
Traditional architecture was often preserved, purely for the want of money to change it. Having usefully served the farmer for several centuries, it now faces an uncertain future. A sympathetic understanding of its past can help to preserve its character for the future.

LEFT: BUILDER'S CRAFT
Flint knapper, thatcher, brick maker, stone dresser, plasterer and carpenter all played their part in the building of this Normandy barn.

NORMANDY

THEY BUILT MONT-SAINT-MICHEL as a monument to God. It became a monument to man. Like the palace of Versailles and the Eiffel Tower, this towered and turreted, Gothic extravaganza is one of the most visited places in the whole of France. Glimpsed from the distant heights above Avranches, it looks a mere sand-castle stranded in the bay, but viewed from the seaside causeway, built in 1879 to save a few souls from drowning, it materializes into a spectacular, multi-tiered, masonry cake, soaring above the sea. At the summit, the gilded figure of St Michael tilts his sword in God's supposed direction and looks down on a striking display of high monastic and low domestic architecture.

A Norman bishop with a sharp eye for a potential investment capitalized on the legendary visit of the Archangel Michael by building a chapel on the summit in AD 709. Work on the monastery continued for centuries, and the townspeople who lived and laboured below were exposed to revolutionary building techniques and the use of some fine, foreign building materials. Nevertheless, when they came to construct their own homes, they fell back on the conservative designs inherited from their forefathers.

The accepted convention, even alongside the contemporary styles of Mont-Saint-Michel, remained true to local tradition. No householder would risk the mockery of his peers by falling for fashion: what was good enough for his grandfather's grandfather had to be good enough for him. And what was good enough for the grandfather was a plain and solid house of stone or wood. The scenic Normandy countryside is full of them.

Normandy's five departments, Seine-Maritime, Eure, Calvados, Orne and Manche, are officially divided between Upper Normandy to the east and Lower Normandy to the west. Seine-Maritime with its white-cliffed seaboard and great chalk flatlands, and Eure, freckled with forests and threaded with rivers, make up Haute Normandie. Basse Normandie covers Calvados, unhappy host to the World War II

LEFT: THE HOTEL AT DEAUVILLE
From the Norman Riviera ports around Deauville and Trouville to the wooded bocage of the west, from the apple orchards of the Pays d'Auge and the deep beech forests of Maine to the wide-open wheat plains of the Pays de Caux, the Normandy landscape is diverse, rich and beautiful. Where local building stone was in short supply, cottages and farmhouses, framed in oak, pattern the landscape. This half-timbered architecture, which survived even the ravages of World War II when over 200,000 buildings were destroyed, has come to symbolize the Normandy countryside.

landings; landlocked Orne, an intimate hinterland of small farms, big forests and discreet stills, and Manche with its snub-nosed Cotentin Peninsula. The area known as the Suisse Normande, which bears little more resemblance to Switzerland than it does to the Gobi desert, covers the uplands of southern Calvados and northern Orne. But the sum of its parts is greater than the whole, for Normandy is a patchworked countryside, a bedspread of little *pays* each with a distinctive identity.

Every spring when *la floréal* breaks out, Normandy wears her Sunday best. In Seine-Maritime's Pays de Bray a lumbering herd of brown and cream cattle amble out on to a buttercupped sward: a quarter of France's cattle chew a Normandy cud. To the north, on the windswept prairies of the Pays de Caux, ant-like processions of tractors tend the wheatfields. In the great forests of the Pays d'Ouche, the winter's wind-felled trees are hauled out and logged up, while in the neighbouring Pays d'Auge gnarled fruit trees run up creamy flags

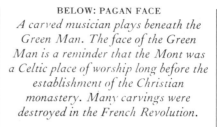

BELOW: PAGAN FACE
A carved musician plays beneath the Green Man. The face of the Green Man is a reminder that the Mont was a Celtic place of worship long before the establishment of the Christian monastery. Many carvings were destroyed in the French Revolution.

RIGHT: BATTLEMENTS
The River Cousenon, whose banks mark the boundary between Normandy and Brittany, meets the sea beneath Mont-Saint-Michel, prompting the Breton saying that Le Cousenon par sa folie a mis le Mont en Normandie *(The Cousenon in its folly has put the Mount in Normandy). The impregnable granite fortifications successfully protected the island against both siege and sea.*

RIGHT: WOOD AND GRANITE
When the great abbey in Mont-Saint-Michel was under construction, building stone came from as far away as the English coast, but the townspeople were content to import only Normandy timber and live in homes built to traditional, local designs.

LEFT: HONFLEUR HARBOUR

The Normans came from Viking stock and Norse names, like the word bec *for a stream, were added to towns and villages across the region. Once the Norsemen had settled and colonized Normandy, they set out from ports like this to conquer distant countries — in 1608, Samuel Champlain sailed from Honfleur to found Quebec in Canada, adding the old Norse suffix to the New World territory.*

RIGHT: TOWN HOUSES IN HONFLEUR

Although the big fishing fleets are no more, the tall houses and cobbled streets of the town, built on the west bank of the Seine, make this one of the best preserved of Normandy's old ports. The sharp light and picturesque surroundings persuaded a succession of nineteenth-century painters, including Corot, Manet, Pissarro, Renoir and Cézanne, to gather at Honfleur.

BELOW: BROKEN ROOF LINES

Until it was superseded by Le Havre, Honfleur was the main port at the mouth of the Seine. Building space in the busy, bustling town was in short supply and houses, five, six and sometimes seven storeys high, were squeezed together.

of blossom above wild primroses and orchids. Nervous farmers sniff the evening air and keep their fingers crossed for a frost-free night.

The character of any landscape is linked to what lies beneath its surface. In eastern Normandy, mountainous deposits of chalk and limestone settled in a warm, soupy sea to be exposed 150 million years later in the crumbling white cliffs of Seine-Maritime. In the west the hard sandstones, slates and granite of the Armorican Massif, a triangle of rock with its nose in Brittany and its foot in the Paris basin, were churned up to form the high ground of the Écouves Forest, Mont des Avaloirs and Suisse Normande.

Geology conditions our existence, dictating the landscapes we live in, the houses we build, even the wealth we accrue. Where the geology changes, the way of life alters with it and the clue to the changes remains fixed in the faces of rural buildings: the big brick and flint farms and barns of the Pays de Caux; the tall seafarers' houses of Honfleur; the warm brownstone of the slated farmhouses by the River

LEFT: NATURAL SUPPLIES
Heavily wooded hillsides provided building timber, while the marshes provided thatchers' reed for the timber-framed houses that run along the ridge overlooking Marais Vernier near the mouth of the River Seine.

LEFT: WEATHERBOARDING
The daub-filled panels between the timber framework needed protection from the elements. Houses would take a coat of plaster and whitewash, while lapped weatherboards were adequate for farm buildings.

BELOW: OVERHANGING EAVES
Thatch has no equal as a roofing material. A roof of reed or straw warmed the occupants, required only the lightest of roof supports, and gracefully rolled around dormers, valleys and wide eaves.

LEFT: PROTECTING THE RIDGE
After the chimney, the most vulnerable part of a thatched roof was the ridge. In Normandy the thatchers protected this with a dressing of clay. Flowers, planted in this rooftop border, helped to keep the clay in place and provided a crest of colour in summer.

RIGHT: THATCHED BARNS
The threshing machine ruined the thatchers' wheat straw and, unless the farmer had a source of good, straight reed nearby, he would have to sharpen up his old reaping hook to cut fresh straw for the farmhouse roof. Gradually tiles and slate took over but, although the new roofing materials did not demand as steep a pitch as thatch, many old buildings still exhibit the distinctive pitch of the thatched roof or toit de chaume *beneath.*

Orne; the limestone windmills of Eure or the terraced rows of thatched and timber-framed cottages of Calvados with a Mohican crest of lilies sprouting from their ridges.

Along the Cotentin Peninsula and around Mont-Saint-Michel, the prevailing stone is granite. Great, creamy-pink chunks of it are lumped into walls and chimneys, bridges and sea defences or run up as a false façade across an older, timber-framed building. The best stone, cut and squared by hand, formed corner-stones and straight edges while the worst was used for rough infill.

The householder who demanded more light to be let into his stone house was a nuisance. The local mason had to find another lintel, another windowsill, another set of carved quoins. There were no such problems with a timber-framed house: windows and doors caused no tension in the basic structure and even resolved the time-consuming task of weaving the wattles into the frame holes.

The simplest and earliest timber frame was formed by pairs of curved timbers, crucks, set out like the frame of an upturned boat. The design was no coincidence, for the Normans come from seafaring stock: when the Romans left, this rolling countryside was settled by a bastard race of Saxon, German and Norse parentage until the Vikings swept in during the early ninth century, beached their broad, wooden boats upon the shore and claimed the country for their own. They called it Northmannia.

This race of boat-builders, who were to set their conquering sails on England, Constantinople, Italy, the Far East and the New World, knew a thing or two about working wood. They knew, or the Anglo-Saxons showed them, how to cleave a hardwood tree in two with a wedge and beetle so that they could form the matching uprights of the cruck frame. Once the frame was formed, a coat of thatch would cover the whole house like a teapot cosy, or the sides were filled with coppiced staves woven into a wall fit for rendering with a pudding mix of whatever came to hand—mud, clay, even dung mixed with animal hair. A good cruck depended on the forester coming up with a naturally arched tree; the later box frame that carried the weight of the roof on a series of smaller, straighter timbers eventually usurped the earlier technique and became the dominant design.

RIGHT: BOURGEAUVILLE
Where the patron could afford the cost, carpenters would decorate the framework with criss-cross and diagonal timbers which served no structural function, but amply demonstrated the craftsmen's skill. Regular coats of limewash were necessary to waterproof the panels between the timbers, but coating the oak beams in paint was a matter of choice — the raw oak needed no protection against the elements.

BELOW: NEW MATERIALS, NEW IDEAS
In the neighbouring Île de France, architects were insisting on the Renaissance style for new domestic and civic buildings. Their influence is seen in buildings like the town mairie *and large houses, like this one near Deauville. Fashionable though it was, with its wrought-iron work, decorative roofline and long windows, it needed metal stays to support the tall chimneys.*

RIGHT: SAINT GERMAIN-LA-CAMPAGNE
Panels between the timbers of this manor house were packed with straw mixed with clay and coated with lime plaster to seal the cracks. Later, brick, stone or, as here, spare roof tiles were mortared in to repair the wattle and daub. In rural areas, the owners of large houses remained content with vernacular styles long after townspeople had adopted the architectural ideas emanating from Paris.

LEFT: SOURCE OF PRIDE
The builders of France's fine country houses would import stone from a considerable distance in order to achieve an agreeable effect. But the use of local stone, taken from the village quarry, ensured that the village church and its houses produced an equally agreeable effect.

To build his house, the carpenter first had to lay his hands upon a good stock of oak, two or three hundred trees of small calibre, some the width of his pot-bellied girth, but most no thicker than his thigh. He purchased his hardwood with the customary caution he employed when buying a winter's supply of Calvados. Before parting with his money, he might drive the tip of his clasp knife into the tight wood to check the sap: was it a good woodland tree, grown close to its neighbours to ensure a tight grain, or was it one of those clay-grown leviathans whose sturdy exterior hid a soft and worthless heart?

Seasoned oak hardens into a nail-bending durability and the carpenter, mindful of the saw doctor's bill, worked the wood fresh and unseasoned. To the wood butcher a beam of green oak is like a piece of cheese which can be cut, shaved, bevelled, carved and pegged with the maximum of skill and the minimum of effort.

The framework was prefabricated off site. Stripped of bark, which went to the nearest leather tanner, the timbers were teased into a complexity of studs and sills, trusses and tie beams. Massive mortice and tenon joints were cut, each joint coded with the carpenter's mark and given a trial fitting before the carter was called to carry the timbers to the building site.

Erecting the skeletal frame required the precision of a viola maker and the bullish strength of a horse butcher to marry up the massive timbers and muscle them into place over a stone plinth. Upper stories were jettied out, a trick which maximized the limited floor space in the crowded streets, although it jeopardized the heads of the pious passing below when the morning chamber pot was emptied.

Door and window openings were slotted into the framework and while glass came early to the monastery, the poorer townspeople had to make do with an oilcloth curtain and a stout pair of weatherproof shutters. The remaining holes were filled with split oak laths, with willow or hazel woven between them like a sheep hurdle. This surface, daubed with mud or clay, could then be limewashed.

Roofs were a perennial problem. Heated disagreements would break out across the café tables in the evening lamplight as one builder boasted the merits of the new compressed mudstones that were being quarried in Brittany while another, mindful of his profit margins, dismissed the newfangled slates and extolled the virtues of a thick reed thatch. Inevitably conservatism ruled the day and the timber merchant stole a march on both mason and thatcher with his plentiful supply of wood shingles.

For all its virtues, the half-timbered house had its faults and the carpenter had a price to pay for building in unseasoned oak. In summer the timbers contracted, opening gaps between the daub and the wood. Less sensitive to draughts than today, the householder filled the cracks with daub or limewash, or took no risks and ran his roof shingles right down the weather face of the building.

The seventeenth-century buildings in places like Mont-Saint-Michel in the west and Forêt Lyons in the east represent some of the best of the timber-frame tradition. Where the patron's purse could take the strain, the carpenter set extra timbers dancing across the façades in kissing criss-crosses and superfluous diagonals, while master carvers

RIGHT: WATER'S EDGE
A sharp rise in the price of timber during the seventeenth century led to a consequent increase in the number of stone buildings. However, where good quality stone was readily available, it was always the preferred material.

RIGHT: CATHEDRALS OF THE COUNTRYSIDE
The dark tiled roofs and light-coloured limestone on these barns at Château d'O near Sées make a kind impression on the local landscape.

formed beatific saints, cherubic angels and growling devils in projecting newels. During the French Revolution, most of these sculptures were crudely hacked from the buildings.

The farmer was not too troubled by either decoration or desecration. All he required was a set of dry walls, a waterproof roof, a good-sized hearth and somewhere weatherproof for his precious animals and crops. Depending on the region, he would adopt the linear approach, housing family, servants and animals under one long low roof with a narrow house door and a second opening the width of the oxen's horns for his stock. In the longhouse he was not so proud that he needed a partition between his cattle and his family although, if his building site sloped, he made sure the liquid by-products of his bovine neighbours drained downhill away from the kitchen. One end of the longhouse, where hemp, herbs or game were hung to dry, he left unwalled, hipping the roof over in that distinctive half-hip which echoed the shape of the protective noseplate on the helmet of the Norman warrior.

Elsewhere he adopted the scattered approach, clustering home, sheds, barns and byres in a meadow which served as farmyard and orchard. If the family outgrew the little timber house, he simply built another next door. In parts of the Pays de Caux two or three domestic buildings (their chimneys give them away) survive in these farmyard orchards, each a little sturdier than the last.

These old farm settlements still pattern the rural infrastructure of the province which explains why walking and cycling in Normandy is more pleasurable than punitive: few villages (or their cafés) are further apart than a dawn walk to work by the *journalier*, the day labourer. But the farmer remained subservient to the agricultural calendar and took an odd-jobbing approach to house repairs. Should a plug of clay dry up and drop out from between a pair of close-studded timbers, he might fill the gap with thin handmade bricks. If madame demanded a proper dairy for cheese making, he might tack a cool shed or outshut on to the back of the farmhouse, roofing it with small clay tiles and cladding the timbers in wooden weather-boarding. If his new cart was too wide for the old stable door, he used it to fetch a load of halved timbers from the woods and popped an extension on to one end of the

house. This time he might cover the roof in diagonal hung, black slate, bartered from a bent boatman who had delivered a short measure to an unsuspecting client up-river.

Such treatment did not detract from the aesthetic delight of the half-timbered house. Nor did it weaken the structure. An oak frame will survive a tornado (a fact of little comfort to the householder since the wind would denude the house of roof and panels) and if a fairy-tale giant were to lift a pegged oak frame from its plinth and stand it on its head, the frame would remain intact.

Some of Europe's oldest inhabited homes are oak built and will outlive their modern concrete counterparts by a safe century or three. Neither is oak an inferior building material ranked above the softwood log cabin, but distinctly beneath the house of stone. This popular fallacy arose in the Middle Ages when the Normandy carpenter lost his reputation as principal craftsman to the church-building stonemasons who made him play second fiddle as their roof builder.

Even a modest carpenter will argue that the timber-frame tradition, brought to perfection in Normandy, is not only as valid a building prototype as anything made of stone but just as beautiful.

RIGHT: A MAJESTIC FARMHOUSE
This three-storeyed building near Camembert blends in with the surrounding landscape. Upwards of 300 trees, most no thicker than the carpenter's thigh, might be used in a building of this size. The timbers would be felled from the local woodlands, fashioned while the wood was still green, and allowed to season when the framework was in place. It was a quick and simple method of construction that did no damage to the environment.

RIGHT: CAMEMBERT
The rural house was more than a place to live: it was a place to work. Here in the Pays d'Auge, farmhouse and barns were clustered around a meadow which served as both farmyard and orchard and, when the family outgrew the old house, they built a new one next door, turning their former dwelling place into a barn or byre or, in this village of cheese, a dairy. No two buildings were identical.

BRITTANY

A QUIET REVOLUTION HAS taken place in rural France over the last fifty years which has caused a more profound change in the countryside than anything else that has happened in the last three centuries. It has brought traditional village life to an end. The village was once our starting point. It gathered our ancestors protectively together into a self-sufficient community which met their social, domestic and employment needs. The annual hiring fair provided a venue for the wealthy to find servants and the less fortunate to find work; the weekly market exported the village produce and imported news, while local gossip was exchanged around the communal wash house and the village pump. Vigilant about close cousins, parents found marriage partners for their children, while the peasant economy provided work and low wages for them all.

In the 1940s, a third of the French working people still lived off the land: forty years later, the figure had dropped to less than ten per cent and it continues to fall. Although the same proportion of the population live outside the major cities as they did a century ago, the rural population is now concentrated in the country towns. After 1,500 years of organic consolidation, the village has been defeated by better jobs, better transport, better shopping and a better nightlife in town. The little country hamlet faces an uncertain future.

The twentieth-century revolution, which transformed an agricultural economy into an industrial one, has turned the hiring fair, the wheelwright, the pig butcher, the cooper, the clog-maker and the miller into features of the recent past, memories to be conjured up by village veterans over a glass of Breton cider.

Among the French provinces, the Brittany countryside fared worse than most. When a village business shut down, the owner closed the shutters, padlocked the door and shuffled away leaving the building to die. Rural depopulation meant that there was no demand for roofs over heads and, as the workers and their families left for the towns, the village school, shop, post office and bar went into a terminal decline. In

LEFT: PAIMPOL

The Breton seaside town, frantic in the summer, soulful in winter, protects itself against the Atlantic with a face of granite and a roof of black Brittany slate. The Bretons themselves are a race of Celts, not Gauls, and have less in common with France than with the scattered Celtic populations of the Irish, Scottish, Welsh and Cornish people to the north. La petite Bretagne, *absorbed into France in 1532, was the last major region to accede to the French crown.*

extreme cases whole communities packed their bags, locked their doors and left. There is no sadder sight in Brittany than the derelict remains of one of these ghost villages.

Brittany's rural population has been defecting to the towns for several centuries, because the Breton inherited a thin soil with a stone-strewn surface. Civic administrators divided up Brittany into the four departments of Île-et-Vilaine, Côtes-du-Nord, Finistère and Morbihan, but the forces of nature imposed the real boundaries. Threads of molten rock, cooled and turned to granite, buttress the jutting snout and jowl of this wolf's head of land against the Atlantic, while the 500 million-year-old triangle of rough rock, the Armorican Massif, holds

the central ground. The Alpine summits of its mountains have been ground down, leaving the highlands of Arrée and Menez in the north and the Montagnes Noires and the Lanvaux moorland in the south. North and south in their turn are separated by a soft basin of rock running inland through Finistère where the landscape lushes out into the *argoat*, the land of woods.

Originally settled by a strange Iberian people, Armorica, as it was called, is peppered with dolmens and menhirs, standing stones and cromlechs left behind by master masons whose sophisticated civilization pre-dates the first Egyptian dynasty by at least a thousand years.

RIGHT: GRANITE SURROUNDS
A Breton house name is carved into the granite lintel above a cottage window. At one time the language varied so much across the region that people in Morbihan would have had difficulty understanding their compatriots in neighbouring Finistère. Despite attempts by early twentieth-century educationalists to rid their schools of the Breton tongue, the language has survived.

RIGHT: A GIANT ROCK GARDEN
Great granite bosses outcrop in a farmhouse garden near Trégastel-plage on the Côte de Granit Rose. The roof is tucked in between neat parapets of triangular stone which culminate in projecting kneeler stones, a favourite feature of this region's buildings. Stocky chimneys, small windows and a roof of slate complete the picture.

LEFT: HANDMADE HOUSE
The stone and woodwork on this Breton building were all shaped with hand tools. Buildings like these were labour intensive and the arched doorway, chamfered stones and notched window lintel represent many hours' work.

In the sixth century BC the Celts settled Armorica, resisting the influence of invading Romans and Gauls, but absorbing a second wave of Celtic immigrants who so thoroughly Christianized the country that the Breton calendar still revolves around church life. They were also the people who nostalgically renamed the province *la petite Bretagne*, Little Britain.

Historically and linguistically, the people of Brittany have less in common with the rest of France than with the scattered Celtic populations of the Irish, Scottish, Welsh and Cornish people. Like their fellow Celts across the sea, they have acquired and preserved a deep-rooted passion for folklore, legend and music. The Breton language is similar to Welsh and, like the Welsh language, suffered the fate of being ruthlessly suppressed by state educationalists. Along with the Breton's defiant sense of identity, the language has not been forgotten but it is no longer the language of the people.

Brittany was the last major region to accede to the French crown and the twist of fate which cost Little Britain its independence could be attributed to the work of a careless stonemason.

The story goes that La Duchesse Anne, Brittany's last reigning sovereign and a champion of Breton rights, was forced into a marriage with the French king, Charles VIII. To everyone's surprise this marriage of inconvenience turned into one of love and respect and the couple slipped off to the royal love-nest at Château d'Amboise on the Loire. Charles was so eager to turn the château into a palace fit for his queen that he had the masons working overtime, building at night by torchlight and heating the stones in winter so that they could still be fashioned. Brittany's sovereignty was safe in the hands of the duchess and her doting husband, but their happily-ever-after story came to an abrupt end when Charles cracked his skull on a low lintel and expired.

The subsequent monarchical machinations ended with his widow married off to the next heir to the throne, Louis XII. Although Anne extracted an assurance that her beloved Brittany would remain an independent state, Louis cared more for the honour of a united France than any matrimonial promise. The conditions were violated and Brittany finally became another piece of mother France, all for the want of a better-placed lintel.

ABOVE: FARMERS AND FISHERMEN
The livelihood of the coastal Bretons depended on drawing a living from both land and sea. At Melon the whitewashed façade of a perfectly proportioned pentwin *looks out to sea.*

The settlement of Brittany, both inland and along its crinkled coastline, was a small-scale affair. Cursed with a poor soil and served by sunken roads so deeply potholed the night-time traveller ran a real risk of drowning, rural communities remained fragmented and isolated. Throughout the *bocage* lonesome houses, built to weather the winter storms, sit in a patchwork of *champs clos* or hedged fields surrounded by raised dykes planted with trees. These basic units were closer to the gruelling realities of self-sufficiency than anything dreamed up by our post-industrial-age escapists.

They grew their own food and made their own entertainment. During long winter nights, neighbours met at each other's houses for the *veillées* or evening gatherings to share a little lace work and tell a story or two. When the host grew tired he would pointedly bring proceedings to a close by heaping ash on the burning fire. The jaw-weary farmers and their families would return in the dark, passing the communal *lavoir*, fishpond, bake oven and mill, to slip latch and lock against the wolves. (Legend records that the wolves who ate Saint Thégonnec's shire horses were forced to pull his plough themselves.)

Place
Prosper Proux
Barde 1811-1873

If wolves have gone the way of the *veillées*, the village well capped with a granite coping stone and the squat bread oven roofed with turf and blackened with age are still a central feature in many a Breton village. It is still possible to eavesdrop on a group of old women clucking dismissively at one of their profligate daughters who has bought a washing machine.

The hard but co-operative way of life of this westerly region, the climate, and the availability of suitable materials conditioned the way the Breton built his house. The basic crofter's cottage, a single-roomed unit built of stone with a turf roof, could be 2,000 years old. Some still show a detectable reddening of the inside walls, a sign that at least once in their long lives they have been fired by marauding brigands.

The Breton *penty*, the low farmhouse, was derived from this primitive rootstock. Walls were thick and broad, wide enough to incorporate pieces of kitchen furniture, a cupboard or a set of cool stone shelves, on the inside walls. In eastern Brittany some were built of mud or rammed earth, finished off with a coating of *torchis* or daub, but the majority were of thickset rubble with big corner-stones. If the

BELOW: BEHIND THE WALL
Finistère, the finis terrae or land's end of western Brittany, is exposed to the wet, windswept Atlantic seaboard. These steep, parapeted roofs, peeping over an ivy-covered wall, may once have been covered in thatch.

LEFT: BUILT TO LAST
The family farmhouse with barn, dairy and cart shed were either grouped close together or, as here near Paimpont, built lengthways with new buildings added on as the need arose. The builder used the lie of the land to the best effect with the farm buildings, which would drain away down the slope, below the farmhouse.

LEFT: INLAND BRITTANY
A patchwork of small fields and isolated farmhouses patterns the interior. In general, the early house builders had to manage with whatever material was locally available, and the vernacular architecture which resulted from their efforts fits kindly into the landscape of undulating hills.

RIGHT: LAND OF WOOD
The argoat, *or land of wood as the interior is known, provided a plentiful supply of building material and many timber-framed buildings, their panels filled with wattle and daub, survived to grace the streets of towns like Josselin.*

RIGHT: TOWN HOUSES
The vernacular tradition drew to a close earlier in the towns and large villages where the householder was more susceptible to fashion than in the remote rural regions. Here at Auray, slate has been run down the weather face of the gable as an extra precaution against the elements.

LEFT: BIRD'S EYE VIEW

The sharp, gabled roofs of Josselin's timbered town houses run down towards the River Oust.

LEFT: OLD AND NEW

The elaborate stonework around a window in Pont-Aven compliments the vernacular influence seen here in the slate hood over the pharmacie *window and the corner-stones kept clean of whitewash.*

householder was relying on his own efforts to build the house, he would call in a skilled craftsman to form quoins or corner-stones and celebrate their lumpy lines by keeping them free of his chalk dust and milk whitewash.

The single room might be extended by adding another room to one end, to house the farmer's pig rather than his family, or the roof rafters rearranged to accommodate a neck-cricking bedroom loft reached by a ladder from the kitchen. A flight of stone steps up the outside gable wall led to a grain store in the loft. Windows were kept small, hearths kept large and, if the sods on the low-pitched roof kept the rain out, the householder was content.

That was until around the eighteenth century when the Brittany countryside began to open up. Amazed by the spacious houses of his neighbours in Normandy and by some of the coastal towns where the affluent whaling fleets and herring boats were moored, the Celtic houseowner started to enlarge his home. The roof, raised and slated, was built big enough to accommodate two upper rooms, each with a neat dormer window and extra windows let into the gable end. Dispensing with the worm-eaten loft ladder, the farmer tucked in a tight staircase beside the hearth. And he would celebrate the rebuilding with a datestone and his name over a window or with a carved lintel or notched granite arch over the low door. Meanwhile, the animals which he had sheltered under his own roof were evicted from the house and quartered in purpose-built thatched or shingle-roofed barns.

New materials and fashionable details filtered slowly up the estuaries and rivers. They emanated from the seaports, open to the world, as the Breton fleets brought in new building materials and lonely sailors brought home foreign wives with novel ideas about how the matrimonial home should look. One householder kept the steep pitch of his thatched roof but replaced the straw with a red roof of Mediterranean tile; another dismissed whitewash as old-fashioned and brewed a red ochre wash from a keg of umber he had picked up cheaply in a Cornish port. Then there were fashionable details like the wrought-iron and glass porch hoods. The Breton skies tend to drizzle and a rash of these porch hoods spread through north-east Brittany to become an indispensable feature not only over every cottage door but, oddly enough, over the family tomb as well.

BELOW: TOWER WINDOW
When the householder replaced his thatched roof with slate, he often used the opportunity to raise the roof line and light the attic space with dormer windows. This tower window in the Côtes-du-Nord echoes the Breton's fondness for dormers.

RIGHT: LANNION
The slate-hung face of many town buildings conceals a timber-framed structure beneath. Until river and road transport improved in the eighteenth century, the use of slate was confined to slate-quarrying districts.

RIGHT: PATTERN OF SLATE
Brittany slate was already being exported to the English south coast in the Middle Ages. Its close texture and resistance to frost made it an ideal roofing and cladding material throughout northern France.

For the family headstone, sawn and polished slabs of Brittany slate could be relied upon to preserve the memories of the dead. Slate, a metamorphic rock squeezed and heated by natural forces into a stone which can be cut and split into wafer-thin slices, was exported from Brittany in the Middle Ages. Before it was replaced by manmade materials, it was used for door lintels, window sills, wall stones, water-tanks, pig-salting benches, fence posts, steps and even cheese presses.

When Brittany slate began to be commercially quarried and replaced the local thatch, the Breton builder made the new material conform to the rounded shape of the old roofs, so that on the neat gites around Josselin, the pink granite buildings of Perros-Guirec or the grand farmhouses of the Pays de Dol, roofs look as if the slate was moulded rather than laid. For extra protection against Atlantic storms, slate was often run down the weather face of the buildings as well; in Lannion they coated the whole façade of a timber-framed building giving it a curious, armour-plated look.

Where the thatched roof has survived, as in the thatched village near Kervignac in southern Brittany, the increasing popularity of Brittany as a place to live rather than leave suggests they are safe for the foreseeable future. For Brittany has experienced a change of fortune: the telecommunications revolution and a considerably improved road network has triggered a building boom in cottage conversions. City people are moving back to the country to compete with German, English and Dutch immigrants who have fallen for the Breton way of life and want to buy into it. Second-home ownership is now higher in France than in any other European country.

So while Breton lace still curtains the farmhouse window, a low-hung Citroën with Parisian plates lurks in the cart barn; the baker's oven still juts out from the side of the old *boulangerie* but, warmed now by central heating instead of charcoal, it houses a tasteful library; the pantiled outshut that was once open to the west winds and festooned with fishing nets is now glassed in and log-jammed with potted begonias and sunny geraniums.

The new incomers may not be able to revive the traditional village life or save flagging rural services, but they may at least rescue a few of Brittany's traditional houses from dereliction.

❧ 4 ❧

BURGUNDY

For a region better known as a label on a wine bottle than a geographical location on the French map, Burgundy is a place people pass through rather than to. They have been doing it for centuries. Midway between the Mediterranean and the French capital, between Italy and northern France, Burgundy became a crossroads, a stop-off point where the traveller waited impatiently for a change of horse or reluctantly took a bed for the night to break a journey from somewhere else to somewhere else.

The Romans drove their road, the Agrippa, through Burgundy to link Rome with the north. The modern motorways, La Comtoise linking Paris and Basle, and the Autoroute du Soleil which follows Agrippa's course, still sluice people through the region's heartland.

The motorists pass, watching the domestic architecture gradually assume a southern feel and glimpsing the occasional Romanesque church perched high on a green hill. In medieval times these churches were decorated with graphic pictures of purgatory, stentorian warnings to the unrepentant which showed their lost souls being cheerfully pitchforked into the fires of hell. A more contemporary version of the afterlife would depict the sinner eternally damned to journey up and down the autoroute, cursed with a full fuel tank, while the blessed were free to wander the quiet lanes of rural Burgundy in peaceful tranquillity and quiet contemplation.

Defining where those leafy lanes begin and end is difficult for Burgundy has a problem with her boundaries. Burgundians will tell you the seat of their province lies in Dijon, that great grey city which gave respectability to multi-coloured roofs and outshone all rivals in the fifteenth century. Dijon was the base for the dukes of Burgundy whose territory ran from the Jura mountains through north-east France to encompass most of Belgium and much of Holland. Shrivelled by the chill of political change to more modest modern dimensions, the Burgundians of today still make the business of delineating boundaries sound like guesswork.

LEFT: TURBULENT HISTORY
Quiet country towns like Beine belie the region's imperial past when the ambitious dukes of Burgundy threatened the nation's rulers. Outmanoeuvred by the French crown, the people of Burgundy settled instead to the serious business of cultivating the land and patterning the landscape with their traditional buildings.

The confusion may be due to their imperial past. Or it may be because, as recently as the late nineteenth century, the people found it difficult to understand one another. Burgundy is composed of dozens of different country areas including Puisaye, Pays d'Othe, Barrois, Nivernais, Amognes, Châtillonnais, La Vôge, Bazois, Brionnais, Charollais, Mâconnais. Each not only possessed its own distinctive identity, but spoke a different dialect.

A foreigner would have been further perplexed by the state tongue: checking he had chosen the right road for Lyons, the traveller would receive an affirmative '*oïl*' in the north, while a southerner would reply '*oc*'. For Burgundy straddled the linguistic division between north and south France, the *langue d'oc* of the south and the *langue d'oïl*, which later became the *langue d'oui*, of the north.

The name Burgundy was only officially revived in 1964 as a catchall for the four departments of Côte d'Or, Saône et Loire, Yonne and Nièvre. The forgotten people who gave the region its original name must have let out a ghostly sigh of relief. The Germanic tribe known as the Burgundiones, who bleached their long locks with lime and conditioned them with rancid butter, ruled a kingdom which took in most of Switzerland and eastern France as far down as Arles.

Long after they disappeared, the second Burgundian empire, this time under the dukes of Burgundy, again threatened to eclipse that of mother France. The loss of their leader, Charles the Rash, who became wolf meat after his abortive winter siege of Nancy in 1477, marked the beginning of the end. The province which had been a thorn in the royal flesh settled to becoming a jewel in the royal crown.

The number of entries given to Burgundy in any good gourmet guide demonstrates how this province enriched the French purse: the province is a byword for good food and wine. The very name Burgundian suggests a well-fed, well-rounded fellow and his domestic architecture manages to mirror both the region's fecundity and its chequered imperial past.

Along the northern boundaries between the Loire and the Seine, municipal buildings bow to the Parisian style. But the local farms and cottages look defiantly east towards all those places that once came under Burgundian rule.

RIGHT: VINEYARD OF FRANCE
Burgundy is closely associated with the wine industry, not least because it possesses more appellations d'origine than the rest of France put together. And yet the Burgundian vineyards occupy only a small proportion of this green and pleasant land: the rest is taken up with lush valleys, gentle hills and a wealth of vernacular architecture.

LEFT: MONASTIC POWER
The influential Benedictine monastery at Cluny was behind the flowering of classical architecture in Burgundy during the eleventh and twelfth centuries. However, the vernacular architecture took its form from the distinctive identities of different pays *like Charollais, Nivernais, Mâconnais and Puisaye.*

LEFT: PEACEFUL SCENE
The honey-brown and red roofs of handmade flat tiles or tuiles plates *and the grey walls of local stone give Collan a serene appearance.*

Hipped roofs, steep-pitched and honey-tiled, grace tall town houses. Broad-shouldered farmhouses, twice as long as their town cousins, stretch out like contented cats beside blood-red cherry orchards and buttercupped meadows. Country villages, purposefully agricultural, wind their roads between neat cottages with barn doors that open on to the street. Along the precious Chablis vineyards, the *vignerons'* or winegrowers' courtyards are framed by the limestone pillars and arched entrances.

The rural architecture also accentuates the north-south divide. A town like Saint Fargeau in the Puisaye, that misty, marshy *pays* brought to prominence by its literary daughter Colette, looks like any stout northerner should: rough stone walls hide beneath a coat of render, clean-cut freestone frames doors and windows, and the surrounds are given a lick of whitewash to make them stand out in the dark. Roofs, slate-shod and upstanding, sit above half-timbered buildings and lead to tall chimneys formed in brick.

But join the promenaders on a summery Sunday evening in the villages of the Charollais or the Brionnais in the south-west and an unmistakable Mediterranean ambiance drifts between shutters opening up after the noonday heat. Roofs are red-tiled, washing hangs in the open house gallery, husks of maize harden in their drying racks and there is even that faint, southern aroma of something unmentionable wafting up from the drains.

What unites Burgundy is the sense of verdant growth that hangs in the drowsy summer air. Fat white cattle browse udder-deep in lush meadows from Senonais in the north to southern Charollais, the *pays* which first bred the breed. Country lanes lined with wild juniper switchback through a merry-go-round of greenery, one moment running between hectares of grain fields and choirs of yellow-faced sunflowers, the next, slipping between heavily-wooded hillsides where cicadas trill and nightingales break the midnight air.

Apart from the hilly Morvan region, the land fattened what the farmer chose while his wife's cooking put the province on the international cuisine scene: *coq au vin*; *boeuf bourguignon*; Dijon mustard (did it really originate from the impatient Philip the Bold's *Il me tard?*); and wine.

BELOW: GLAZED TILES
The coloured roofs of country houses in and around Dijon were made with patterns of glazed tuiles plates. Purely decorative and made to order, the tiles were rarely used on the roofs of vernacular buildings.

RIGHT: REFLECTIONS OF PROSPERITY
In Mirabeau, north-east of Dijon, substantial houses and warehouses line the waterfront. The commercial combination of good harvests and a river or canal to export the harvests brought affluence to the farming communities.

An uncharitable view holds that the wine only became popular because foreigners could pronounce Chablis, Chambertin, Pommard and Mâcon. But the Burgundy brew is exceptional and the province possesses more *appellations d'origine* than the rest of France put together. Grapes grow on Côte vineyards, sloping hillsides, well drained and bone dry, and the vineyards snake out along a limestone ridge, stretched like a washing line between the granite massifs of the Vosges in the north-east and Morvan in the south-west.

The wine, variously regarded as a luxury, a hazard to health and the only way to start the day, has given economic sustenance to the region for nearly 2,000 years. The procession of historical figures who cultivated the grape include Gauls, Romans and, in the eleventh and twelfth centuries, the monks of the Cluny Order in the south and the Cîteaux Order in the north. The monks, and the wine barons that followed them, constructed huge buildings to process and store the wine. In the absence of a subterranean cellar, walls were two feet thick, windows were small and floors and ceilings were insulated with a mixture of sand, dry moss and clay.

BELOW: STEEP PITCH
The sharp slope of local roofs is a typical feature of the Burgundy house. Before clay tiles became widely available, roof coverings were of thatch or stone tiles.

LEFT: BASIC BUILDINGS
The Morvan district was far less fertile than the rest of Burgundy and domestic buildings were correspondingly smaller and more basic. This tiled roof in Quarré-les-Tombs was probably thatched until the mid-1950s when mechanical harvesters deprived the thatcher of his roofing material.

LEFT: COUNTRY AUBERGE
The timbered upper floor of the Auberge de la Quatr'Heurie at Bèze is a rare example of half-timbered work in this neat, limestone village.

Come the revolution and everything changed. Prosperous owners lost their holdings and the vineyards were sold on and divided up among the new republicans. A change in the law of primogeniture meant older sons had to share their slice of the booty with younger brothers. Even today an average holding on the Côte de Beaune south of Dijon is no more than a couple of acres.

White grapes are pressed when they are picked. The red must first be brewed in great vats. The new republican vintners had been in feudal service for generations and knew all about growing and making wines: what they lacked was a place to prepare it and a cellar to store the bucolic fruits of their labour. They responded by adapting traditional designs and quarrying local stone to meet the new need. If the same process had taken place in the twentieth century, uniform designs and standardized materials would have blighted the landscape: as it was, each wine district developed its own distinctive wine house.

In the Côte d'Or, for example, vats and presses were incorporated into an outshut or adjoining shed. The humble living quarters (a kitchen and bedchamber were still sufficient for a family's needs in the

RIGHT: WINEMAKER'S HOUSE
The vineyards of Burgundy evolved their own particular architecture, designed or adapted to suit the different processes involved in the manufacture of wine. In the Chablis region at Fleys, stone, dressed and chamfered, frames the doorway of a barn built to the dimensions of a fully loaded cart.

BELOW: AVALLON
The tiled roofs and solid stone façades of the old town, perched on a rocky spur overlooking the River Cousin, give Avallon an unmistakeably Burgundian look.

RIGHT: HIDDEN TIMBERS
Comparative affluence in the seventeenth and eighteenth centuries gave the people of Burgundy the opportunity to follow the architectural styles of the neighbouring Île de France. One favourite technique was to conceal exposed timbers beneath a stone face or a render of sand and lime.

eighteenth century) were housed on an upper floor over the cellar and reached by an outside flight of steps. An open gallery, hung with the house vine, sheltered the stairs.

Down in the Mâconnais, cellar and harvest equipment were tucked in next door to each other at ground level. Since cellar temperature was critical—between ten and fifteen degrees centigrade—the living quarters still sat protectively over the wine store like a partridge over her chicks. Unless the farmhouse was built on a hillside, and a cellar cave could be hollowed out beneath the building, an insulating bank of earth was shovelled up against the outside of the cellar walls.

A series of good vintages allowed the *vigneron* to improve his property, to gather the working buildings around a central courtyard, extend the gallery to catch the early sun, or test the blacksmith's skill by ordering a pair of painted iron doors. Despite the vagaries of viniculture, phylloxera epidemics or an inexplicable change in taste for white or red wine, the *vigneron* has prospered. His village, little changed in two centuries, has an air of unobtrusive affluence, the result of a seven-day working week spent nursing the grape to fruition.

One successful enterprise creates a satellite of dependent businesses: as one seventeenth-century traveller complained, Nuits-Saint-Georges had 'but one good main street which is however inhabited only by coopers'. The blue-smocked, migrant carters known as *galvachers* from neighbouring Morvan were among the beneficiaries.

The Morvan rises like a great granite lump 600 metres above the Burgundy countryside. Heavily wooded and sprinkled with silvery lakes and remote hamlets, it yielded a reluctant living to its people and many Morvandiaux spent their time in exile, seeking work. Among them, in the nineteenth century, were the *galvachers* who left with their ox carts in March and returned the following November. These latter-day road hauliers, who often sold the ox and cart in the autumn and returned on foot, would set off along the Paris road each spring, the mud lapping over the tops of their clogs, their ox carts loaded with local wine and firewood for the capital. As they rumbled along, they would pass Parisian babes in arms heading for the Morvan to be breast-fed by their own wives: suckling children was not considered a ladylike activity among the high-born Paris women.

LEFT: MATCHING BLUE
An unglazed opening, let into the wall to circulate air through the old stable and cart shed, provides a niche for a colourful plant on this house near Chablis.

BELOW: STONE HARVEST
Jurassic limestone in the vineyards of Mâconnais, yields a perfumed white wine from the Chardonnay grapes. These same stones were quarried and cut to form the buildings in towns and villages like Saint Gengoux-le-National.

LEFT: METAMORPHOSIS
Straddling an imaginary border between the south and north of France, the folk architecture of Burgundy gradually changes from Roman-tiled and open-galleried houses in places like Cluny, to cold climate buildings like this half-timbered and slate-roofed house in Saint-Fargeau.

RIGHT: FALSE FRAMING
The fashion for exposed half-timbered work has swung back and forth. In the nineteenth century the timbers on the outside of buildings were being busily concealed behind false façades; a hundred years later false beams were being incompetently painted across the face of good stone buildings.

toute
heure

BAR

LEFT: RIPE FOR RENOVATION
A farm building records how handmade bricks were occasionally used as infill between the timber framework. Repairs to the roof have given this barn a new lease of life.

RIGHT: STABLE DOOR
Carefully selected, cut stone has been employed to form the frame around this barn door. The use of a whitewash on the surrounds assisted the farmer, returning from work late at night, to find the stable door in the dark.

BELOW: LA FERME DU CHÂTEAU
Recognizing the importance of vernacular architecture, many regional eco-museums re-create both the buildings and the way of life of rural communities. Stone quoins, limewash, timber cladding and handmade bricks appear side by side in the buildings of this working farm museum at Saint-Fargeau.

The Morvan women's clothing was the antithesis of Paris fashion. Dressed in woollen cloth with broad stripes, wool stockings and clogs with skeepskin uppers, they covered their heads with broad quilted calico bonnets. And the city-born babes found themselves being weaned in cottages that were as much a lesson in economy as their own homes were a lesson in lavishness.

Like their counterparts in Brittany, these one-storey houses sit low on the land, tucked into a hillside or huddled together for companionship. And yet, although they shared the same rough stone and a similar topography, they developed their own characteristic form. On the lower floor a kitchen-come-bedroom, built round the open hearth, butted up to the barn and byre where the Morvan cattle, hardy black animals, and the oxen were stalled. An attic, built on chestnut or oak joists, stored fodder and was cooled by the flow of air passing through two or three thin, machinegun-like slits tucked under the thatched eaves. Slate replaced thatch when mechanical combines and silage cutters deprived the thatcher of his basic material after World War II.

The impoverished house builder inherited an equally impoverished stone. The local mason would call to form the quoins, and door and windows surrounds in grey and pink granite, while the houseowner laboured to build the walls in between, sometimes leaving throughs, long stones laid in the random rubble for extra stability, jutting out of the gable walls.

The superstitious held that a red raddle on the house kept the devil at bay, but in the Morvan coats of limewash, with pink, brown, yellow or orange pigment added in, waterproofed the rough walls, although it was carefully contoured around the exposed granite work.

The *vigneron's* house and the humble cottages of the Morvan are but two of the different vernacular styles that developed in Burgundy. A province with so many *pays* naturally evolved an equally diverse housing stock—to trace them all requires detailed detective work. But wherever you look in the Burgundy countryside you are likely to find an equally curious pair of eyes gazing back at you over the hedge: the bored Charollais, affectionately known as *les vaches qui regardent les trains* (the cows who watch the trains), like to know what is going on.

RIGHT: CANAL MOORINGS
The Burgundy waterways, like the Canal de Bourgogne at Tanlay, not only exported the province's rich produce, but also imported the cheap, mass-produced building materials which eventually brought the vernacular traditions to an end.

❧ 5 ❧
PROVENCE

PROVENCE IS AS BEAUTIFUL as it is diverse and a long day's drive from one end of the province to the other would reveal it as a land of incomparable contrasts. The journey would begin at dawn among the frog-croaking marshes of the Camargue, pass by the peach trees and melon beds of the lower Rhône valley, the bright, barren crags of Mont Ventoux and the bulky, white whaleback of Mont Sainte-Victoire, which figured in so many of Cézanne's paintings. Continuing east, the traveller would slip between red-roofed, hilltop villages, blue-green olive groves and purple lavender fields, past the sparkling Mediterranean and on, via the extravagant flower gardens that feed the scent factories of Grasse, to finish at sunset high up among the snow-capped peaks of the Alps.

Such an epic journey would exhaust the traveller and deprive him of the hidden pleasures of Provence—the smell of a pine wood, the peace of the siesta, an evening game of boules—but it would give credence to the local version of creation: when God finished planet earth he discovered he had some pieces left and decided to fashion them into a miniature paradise. They called His paradise Provence.

'Provence' actually comes from the Latin *Provincia*, tamed by the Romans around 125 BC so as to provide a safe passage between Rome and its Iberian territories. While Rome's *Provincia* embraced the whole of southern France from the Alps to the Pyrenees, today's boundaries run from the Italian border to Languedoc in the west.

When the Romans withdrew, leaving behind their rich architectural remains, the people of Provence fell prey to any tribe that happened to be passing: Franks, Goths, Visigoths, Burgundians, Saracens and Normans all came, saw and conquered. The Provençaux treated each new arrival with the same resigned equanimity they currently display to the annual invasion of one and a half million holidaymakers.

Religion rather than politics upsets the Provençaux. The *guerres de religion* produced some spectacular barbarities but, for the most part, the people quietly continued nurturing the land and harvesting the sea

LEFT: MEDITERRANEAN LIGHT
The use of bright colours for limewashing the outside of buildings, aesthetically risky in the misty north of the country, was eminently suitable in the sparkling, clear light of Provence. Here at Roussillon and the neighbouring village of Rustrel, pigment from the local rocks coloured and waterproofed the buildings.

for surpluses of fish, wine, vermilion, oranges, olives, peppers, dates and cane sugar. By the sixteenth century nearly half the population had acquired a holding of their own and absentee landlords would return to find their land being assiduously cultivated by a neighbour.

A serious blow to Provençal culture was the sixteenth-century decree that all administrative law would be translated from the Latin into the *langue d'oil* rather than Provençal or the *langue d'oc*. Again the people did not seem too troubled if they could not understand the lawyers: the Provençaux, who speak as eloquently with their hands as with their voices, kept their language alive in the market place.

The promise of sea, sun and a painter's light has made a tourist trap of Provence and, although the summer visitor may see the province as a paradise populated by a good-natured people, the local climate can be less than kind. The combination of a hot Mediterranean sea in the south, high Alps in the east and the thermal corridor of the Rhône passing down the west side causes long, hot summers when irrigation channels dry up and a stray spark can lead to devastating destruction.

BELOW: SOLAR PROTECTION
Small windows, tight shutters and a shady grove of olive trees are common features throughout the Mediterranean. The design of the domestic architecture was dictated, not by outward appearances, but by the climate.

RIGHT: SABLAT
The Provençal weather is unpredictable. Scorching summers, freezing winters and an annual rainfall that can exceed that of northern France meant building homes that were weatherproof and waterproof.

RIGHT: LES BAUX
The material that fortified the householder against the worst of the weather was the local stone. The backbone of the Alpilles ridge between Arles and Saint Rémy provided the building materials for Les Baux as well as the mineral Bauxite, mined in the neighbouring hills.

Unexpected frosts sometimes ruin the southerly crops and, when the rain falls, it gushes down in rat-drowning quantities: the annual rainfall in Marseilles is higher than in Paris. Then there are the surprise storms which hurl down hailstones big enough to bruise and winds like the mistral which blow with such steady vehemence they send the locals into temporary hibernation.

The proverbs and prayers of Provence ('Praise the sea—but stick to the dry land', and 'Dear God, let me catch enough fish today to eat, sell, give away and be robbed') suggest a cautious people resigned to

fate. When any of these climatic extremes strikes, they wisely retreat indoors and wait for it to pass. Naturally enough they built their homes with the worst of the weather in mind.

The yellow stone, two-storey cottage or *cabanon* was the Provençal prototype, unless one includes southern France's equivalent of the igloo: *les bories* or *les cabanons pointus* were built entirely in dry stone with roofs formed by corbelling the stone until it met in the middle. It is a primitive roofing solution to which the most sophisticated domed architecture owes its origins. There were disadvantages to living in a single round room and, although it offered more creature than human

RIGHT: UTILITARIAN FARMHOUSE
The Provençal farm was often built around a dependable water supply with the farm buildings centred on the well. The layout of farm and farm buildings depended on both the lie of the land and local custom. Some, like this one beneath Mount Ventoux near Venasques, were concentrated around a courtyard in a U or L shape, others ran lengthways along the country roads.

RIGHT: SOUTH FACING
Where the farm was built lengthways, the house was orientated so that the front, shaded by an open verandah and a house vine, faced the sun, while the back provided some defence against the mistral. The straightforward, double- or single-pitched rectangle of roof was ideal for the Roman tiles which were difficult to lay around complicated valleys or hipped roofs.

comfort, the plain *cabanon* took precedence. Everything from the farmer's family to his tools and beasts found a place to stay in its low-ceilinged, cool interior. Built on the village outskirts, the south-facing *cabanon* wore either a conventional gabled roof or a single pitch sloped up to a north wall. This wall, protected by a row of cypress trees, was the family's defence against the north winds and was left blind, the door and small windows being set in the south side.

Building stone, *lauzettes*, came straight from the surrounding fields and was placed in piles to season while the land was cleared for planting. If he was lucky the *paysan* might find some good carvable blocks for corner-stones and lintels, otherwise it meant a trip to the local *carrière* for quarried stone. In certain districts the local stone was fine enough to split into roof tiles and floor slabs, but generally the roofs took the *tuile romaine* or *tuile à canal*, the handmade, tapered, clay tile, laid in undulating rows, one face up, one face down. Coloured according to the local clay from a dark red to a burnt orange, the tiles eventually bleach out to a uniform pale ochre. Since roofs were sloped at a gentle forty to forty-five degrees, the tile often took no fixing nails or pegs and a *cabanon* that has suffered a strong gust of wind will show a freckling of red, replacement tiles on the pale roof.

The *paysan* was resistant to change, but in the eighteenth century he did adopt the Italian masons' habit of inserting from one to four rows of tiles into mortar beneath the eaves in what was called the *génoise* frieze. This partly decorative design performed the practical function of projecting the last row of roof tiles out from the building so that in a heavy storm, the cascade of rainwater fell well clear of the façade.

The basic *cabanon* influenced the style of the *mas*, the *grange* and that Provençal version of a château, the *bastide*. (In Provence a *bastide* refers not only to a hill town but also to large houses originally found in the countryside around Marseilles.)

No two French villages are identical, but they share common characteristics. A community which lived by the plough spread itself out, while one which struggled to survive in an inhospitable environment kept competing neighbours at a distance and remained scattered and isolated. Where the vineyards ruled and every piece of suitable land grew the grape, the village was concentrated in a dense,

From the Camargue to the Alps, the variety of different landscapes gave rise to a diverse range of buildings. At one extreme are the single-storey, thatched cabins of the Camargue with their chimney, ridge and aspidal end covered in a protective coat of clay.

RIGHT: ALPINE BARN
The design of a barn in the Alps, 2,000 metres above sea level, draws on the local vernacular style with its rough stone walls under a weathertight roof of wood shingles.

serviceable mass. Elsewhere the rural community settled solidly around a dependable supply of spring water or sprawled out along a lucrative trade route.

But the villages of Provence fall into every conceivable category from the straggling Alpine hamlet to the spreading villages of the plains; from the former fishing ports of the Côte d'Azur congregated around yacht-stuffed quays to cosy medieval hill villages clustered around cobbled streets the width of a pair of oxen.

Along the coast and down the Rhône valley, settlements follow the pattern of a pebble dropped in a pond. At the centre is the *village perché* looking down on lowland farms radiating out in a series of circles. These are the *mas* or *grange*, homes to the sixteenth-century settlers who turned the former wasteland into a rich agricultural resource. Depending on local tradition, they nestle around a *cour* or courtyard in a U or L shape, or lie in a line, strung out along the road, blind backs to the mistral, vine-bowered fronts to the sun. Despite the *paysan's* inherent pessimism, these rings of farms prospered with each period of political peace and quiet.

RIGHT: MOUNTAIN VALLEY
Roadside and hedgerow trees in a valley near Pra-Loup are the vestigial remains of the Provençal forests which, until the Roman era, covered most of Provence. The lack of timber led to stone becoming the predominant building material.

The farmer, nevertheless, did not rush to change things and over the centuries the *mas* remained a modestly upmarket version of the *cabanon*. The arched entrance to the courtyard and any surrounding walls were protected, not decorated, with rows of tiles. Doors, windows and porthole-shaped vents were put in the rough walled house where the farmer needed them rather than where they looked architecturally correct.

Inside, the brazier over which old women used to hoist their skirts for a little primitive central heating was replaced by a proper fireplace and this hearth became the central feature in the long, low *pièce de vivre* where the family washed, cooked and ate. Above it, tucked up close to the chimney, was the small family bedroom where the snores of the sleepers competed with the cooing pigeons in their loft beneath the eaves. The braying mule and the bleating goats shared the outhouses with the farmer's poultry, while crops were stored in the loft above.

The farmer was not averse to a little decoration, a *cadran solaire* or sundial, a wrought-iron gate, perhaps some ashlar stone if, like the builders at Brianconnet on the Esteron, they could recycle stone from old Roman ruins.

The *bastide* on the other hand was the nearest thing to a fashionable dwelling house. The setting for the *bastides* which proliferated in the seventeeth and eighteenth centuries was determined not by a convenient water supply but by a convenient view. Correct aesthetics reigned supreme.

Long french windows were carefully positioned around a central door, ground plans adhered to a strict square with twelve- or twenty-metre sides, or a rectangle, twenty metres by ten metres. A quarter of the floor space could be taken up by a grand staircase which led up to the principal rooms: bedroom, boudoir, library and lavatories, the latter a clear statement of rank over the lower orders for whom the privy or the great outdoors was considered sufficient. External walls were ashlar stone and the *génoise*, eventually deemed a vulgarity, was replaced by a cornice. For all their fashionable finery, these grand, old houses remained essentially Provençal, with their tiled roofs peeping over the cornices and their wallstone mirrored in the sunburnt rock of the distant towns and villages.

LEFT: LA GÉNOISE
The génoise *frieze, imported by Italian stonemasons in the eighteenth century and adopted by the Provençaux, is seen here beneath the eaves of a building near Murs. Two or three rows of tiles were set in mortar beneath the roof line which was projected over the top of them. The frieze not only gave the houses a certain elegance, but also served the practical purpose of jettying rainwater clear of the building.*

RIGHT: RUNNING WATER

Although the average annual rainfall in Nice is 750 millimetres compared with 560 millimetres in Paris, the region suffers from long, dry spells. Villages like Séguret could only be established where a spring or well promised a steady supply of water.

BELOW: SUN DIAL

Covering walls with a decorative coat of slaked lime mixed with pigment and water was a regular chore. The limewash not only brightened the house front, but also temporarily sealed any cracks or blemishes.

RIGHT: HILLTOP VILLAGES

Villages perchés, *like Séguret, cluster around the summits of limestone hills near Dentelles de Montmirail. Continuously occupied since medieval times, the limestone houses crowd in on alleyways no wider than a pair of passing oxen.*

LEFT: NARROW ALLEYS
*Built when the need arose, and
improved when the pocket permitted,
the houses of Ménerbes paid less heed
to the architectural conventions of
symmetry than to the pressing need to
make the most of the limited space of
their hilltop building sites.*

Here tall, cool, labourers' homes and their communal wash houses, wells and boules courts were wedged together among narrow cobbled streets. In the poor quarters sliced stone took the place of cut granite, making the cushioned sole of an espadrille essential footwear. Whenever the villagers profited from their feudal lords' prosperity, they celebrated with a rash of home improvements, marking the year they added an upper storey, or built a narrow staircase to replace the loft ladder, with a carved datestone over the doorway.

Local datestones, mostly around the seventeenth and eighteenth centuries, give no clue to when the building was first erected. Dating traditional folk architecture is impossible without a painstaking search through local records and many were simply put up when the need arose, improved when the pocket permitted and changed beyond recognition when they passed out of the ownership of a local working family. (The popularity of Provence has led to many an old hill house being completely gutted and rebuilt around its ancient, but misleading doorway datestone.)

In the Alps too, they were fond of datestones. The mountain people enjoyed their heyday when road and railway began to open up the interior, when they could at last distance themselves from the incestuous business of self-sufficiency, export a little produce and import a little new blood: lowland goats, bulls and wives were sought-after commodities.

Eighteenth- and nineteenth-century datestones, sometimes accompanied by a carving of the occupant's trade, a stone *sabot* or an apothecary's bottle, mark periods of prosperity when walls of river stone received a fresh colour wash in burnt umber, sienna yellow or mellow cream, or a new set of shutters, pierced with a pine-shaped peep-hole, were hung over windows. The house was capped with a deep-eaved roof of fresh softwood shingles or glazed tiles with fish-scale edges and finished off with new timber snow guards, hung beneath the square-capped chimneys. Without these snow checks, the careless or bad-tempered slamming of a front door would cause a minor avalanche.

A favourite Alpine feature was the sun clock: *Mortels, vos plaisirs sans nombre se perdent avec mon ombre* (Mortals, your countless

RIGHT: PROVENÇAL PINK
Subtle colour washes and painted shutters contrast with the ice-capped mountains that surround this Alpine village.

RIGHT: ALPINE VILLAGE
Places like Saint-Sauveur-sur-Tinée, once dependent on relatively primitive farming practices, went into decline around the turn of the nineteenth century. But the tourist industry which so blighted the local architecture on the Côte d'Azur has, with its ski resorts, brought rural regeneration to the Alpine economy.

ABOVE: LITTLE BARCELONA
Barcelonnette was founded by a Catalan count in the thirteenth century. The curiously Latin-American look of the buildings was due to the good offices of three local brothers who emigrated to Mexico and returned much of their subsequent wealth to the town. A proliferation of eighteenth- and nineteenth-century doorway datestones marks the period of rebuilding.

LEFT: ITALIAN INFLUENCE
A former border town between France and Savoy, Entrevaux, with its fortified bridge across the River Var, suggests a cross-fertilization between French and Italian architecture.

LEFT: GUILLAUMES
The Alpine chalet was the prototype from which village houses like these at Guillaumes developed. Low-pitched roofs with wide eaves allowed a blanket of snow to settle in winter and insulate the buildings.

pleasures are lost with my shade) reads the inscription on a sun clock dated 1815 in Thorame-Haute, beneath Montagne de Chamatte.

Outside the village, the chalet farms were designed so that everything from milking the cow to getting at the log pile could be performed under one roof. They turned their backs to the worst weather and their galleried fronts to face the sun and tried to hold a wintery peace with each other until spring released them. Life in the tight confines of a mountain village, where rickety upper galleries were within spitting distance of one another, must have been even more claustrophobic, and feuding neighbours would yearn for warmer weather when they could leave for the wide open spaces of the mountain pastures and the comparative peace of their high altitude *cabanes*. Mostly lost today amongst the ski resort chalets, these little barns, butted into the mountainside, took a lower entrance for the cow-belled cattle and goats and an upper door for the farmer and his store of summer hay.

Despite the modern tendency to reroof in tin, the traditional Alpine home has lasted well, not least because these old houses will survive a serious avalanche which reduces the twentieth-century lookalike chalets to matchwood. Avalanches aside, the rise of comfort and fashion had a direct bearing on the lifespan of vernacular styles. If it was no longer fashionable for the farmer and his family to live above the cows, he evicted the cattle and converted the byre for his own use. If the building was inflexible, he pulled it down and started again.

In the Camargue the demand for a bit of family privacy almost rendered the local *cabane* extinct. The single-storey hut, its reed roof ridged with whitewashed clay, was built like a ridge tent with a bell end. In camping terms the interior of the *cabane* offered the same space as a large caravan, and yet there are records of up to eighteen members of one family living quite happily in one *cabane*, sleeping back to back in the apsidal end and fighting one another for feeding space in the single living room. They might have continued to live in this way had they not been persuaded that it was *de rigueur* to possess separate bedrooms and sanitary arrangements. But the *cabanes*, so simple to erect, were just as easily removed: they disappeared in their thousands earlier this century.

RIGHT: FOOTBRIDGE
The road and upper floor of a village farm building in Bonnieux are joined by a bridge. There was no need to waste the limewash, which protected and decorated the adjoining house, on the bare stonework of the barn.

DORDOGNE

WHILE THE PRECEDING chapters have explored the traditional buildings of four major regions, Normandy, Brittany, Burgundy and Provence, the final chapters are devoted to two sharply contrasting styles found in the one region of Aquitaine. Aquitaine in the south-west of France runs from the mouth of the Gironde estuary down to the Pyrenees and encompasses Dordogne, Gironde, Landes, Lot-et-Garonne and the Pays Basque in Pyrénées-Atlantiques. It is a broad and bountiful sweep of land which embraces not only France's largest forest and Europe's highest sand dune, but also shelters within its folded hills, rolling plains and vast pine plantations the timber-framed and mud smallholdings of the Landais shepherd, the brownstone cottages of Armagnac, the wine-makers' houses of Bordeaux, the great, graceful farmhouses of the Pays Basque and the weathered limestone buildings of Dordogne.

Guidebooks devote more column inches to Dordogne than to any other part of Aquitaine and, since these guides have the onerous task of including at least some of its eight hundred churches, forty-eight prehistoric caves and over a thousand castles and châteaux, the traditional architecture tends to be described in the briefest terms of endearment. The use of expressions like 'the rustic charms of the Périgourdin houses' gives an impression of unity and homogeneity. Nothing could be further from the truth.

The diversity of the local building styles is the result of the extraordinary diversity of the landscape: Périgord Vert and Périgord Noir, Ribéracois and Bergeracois, the Double and Périgord Blanc. Dordogne is bounded by Haute-Vienne, Corrèze, Lot, Lot-et-Garonne, Gironde and Charente, and the people who built their homes here paid less attention to the neat dividing lines between neighbouring departments and more to what lay beneath their feet. Consequently, slate and rough stone was used in the north-east, sandstone in the east, flagstone and limestone in the south-east, timber frame and brick in the west and ochre-coloured stone in the south.

LEFT: RURAL ROUTES

A grand old farmhouse nestles among wooded valleys near Hautefort. The rivers Dronne, Dordogne, Isle and Vézère each thread their way through this department, but post-revolutionary administrators chose to rename the former province of Périgord after the River Dordogne. The new name is still resisted by the farmers who continue to call themselves Périgourdin.

Aquitaine showing Dordogne and Pays Basque

DORDOGNE

Bordeaux · Périgueux · Bergerac · Sarlat

Dordogne

Garonne

PAYS BASQUE

When, following the French Revolution, the old province of Périgord was renamed after one of France's longest rivers, the Dordogne, local people resisted the change. They continued to describe their province as Périgord and themselves as Périgourdin. But they have welcomed other changes: the gentle charms of the department have attracted tourists and brought an influx of new settlers, mostly English and Dutch immigrants, and they have been glad of the extra income to supplement the agricultural economy. Down the centuries, the life of the Périgourdin farmer has been fraught with catastrophes.

During the nineteenth century, when just under ninety per cent of the people were employed on the land, a quarter of the cultivated ground was devoted to vines. Then, in 1868, a disastrous epidemic of phylloxera struck and within twenty years the vineyards were virtually wiped out. For some, rescue came when government controls on the growing of tobacco were relaxed: Dordogne is now the second largest producer in France. For others, it was a matter of sitting out the crisis and praying that alternative sources of income would see them through. In many cases they did not. Over the next fifty years, thousands of Périgourdins deserted the countryside and, despite the current demand for property, a considerable number of old holdings, deserted during this time, still lie derelict.

A century earlier, a similar fate befell the Périgourdin ironmasters when more advanced methods of production put the majority of the foundries out of business. Iron ore has been quarried and smelted in Périgord since the Romans occupied Aquitaine and ironmaking developed into the most significant industry in the department during the seventeenth and eighteenth centuries, due largely to the lucrative armaments trade. Many a Dordogne château owes its good looks to the foundry owners' profits and the price of cannon.

It was ironic that they should have benefited from the manufacture of arms, since they had themselves come under fire so often in the previous two hundred years. Périgord was a perpetual war zone during the One Hundred Years' War when the English, who occupied neighbouring Gironde, battled with the French to gain control of the province. It was to suffer yet again during the Wars of Religion and the peasants' uprising of 1637, but the ravages of war were as nothing

RIGHT: THE DRYSTONE BORIE
The region is well furnished with fashionable châteaux and yet an extraordinary number of these humble stone shelters survive. They show, in their straightforward simplicity, a fine and masterful use of stone. The roof stones, tilted slightly to keep out the rain, were lapped, one on top of the other, until they met at the summit.

compared to the ravages of disease: in 1693, the plague killed about a third of its people. A decade later, hundreds of peasants died of starvation when the harvests failed.

'The ploughmen at their work have neither sabots or stockings to their feet,' noted one eighteenth-century commentator, astonished at the region's poverty. History tends to be generous when recording the vicissitudes of the wealthy, but tells us little about the conditions of the peasants. Historical sources are also vague when it comes to recording the skills of the architect-builder. 'We are well informed about the dwellings of the nobility, but know little of the houses of the middle and lower classes,' wrote Pierre Lavedan in *French Architecture*.

'This is largely due to the fact that the former, for which more money was available, were better built and therefore have lasted better.' It is a questionable assumption. While Périgord is discreetly patterned with vernacular buildings, some of the more ostentatious efforts of the nobility are half their age and twice as dilapidated.

One of the earliest and more curious examples of this long-lasting vernacular architecture is the *borie*, variously described as a shepherd's

LEFT: HAUTEFORT
The architectural qualities of the grand house, however carefully designed to ape the Parisian fashion, could not avoid an acquiescent nod towards the Périgourdin character with their use of local materials. However, buildings like this one, beneath the château at Hautefort, influenced traditional house builders to include elements like the génoise frieze beneath the eaves of vernacular houses.

LEFT: FINE FINISH
The masons' ability to work stone to a fine finish was increasingly used in town houses. Here at Brantôme the ashlar stone and rounded arch with its carved keystone gives an elegant finish to the doorway.

hut, a ground-level cellar or simply a shelter. The *borie* is a rounded, dry stone construction with a domed roof made by corbelling the stone in, layer upon layer, until it meets in a peaked summit. A number certainly do possess sheep-high doorways, but there are many others which are spacious enough inside to house a peasant and his family, given the conditions under which they lived.

The *bories* occur mainly in the wide limestone belt that courses down through Périgord and which is responsible not only for the spectacular escarpments and plateaux or *causses*, and for the network of deep caves which harboured the famous prehistoric engravings and paintings, but also for the honey-yellow colouring which graces so much of the indigenous building.

Wedged between the western seaboard and the eastern high ground of the Massif Central, the ground rocks of Périgord graduate through three geological bands running diagonally from north-west to south-east: clays and sands to the west, the worn and weathered limestone in the centre and rough slate and shale to the east. Each stratum presented a different landscape and yielded a different kind of living.

In the Nontronnais, the northern area known as Périgord Vert, the granites and schist subsoil gave a Limousin-like landscape of damp meadows (the subsoil holds water well) and chestnut woods where the economy depended on the products of the woodlands: cabinet making, cooperage and carpentry. South-east of Nontron, the little town where they make penknives small enough to fit inside a walnut shell, is the more intensively farmed sandstone countryside around Hautefort. This is a land of vines, cherry orchards and market gardens, where, following the birth of a girl, it was traditional practice to plant a walnut tree to serve as her dowry when she came of age. It is also a place which emphasizes the lack of conformity in the *maison périgourdine*.

In villages like Villac, where the old ox-butchering stall still stands in the main street, the walls of old red sandstone have weathered to the warm brown colour of the soil and the sharp-pitched slate roofs are pierced with hooded openings to ventilate crops stored in the attic. The trouble with the sandstone was that it crumbled away under the effects of frost and on several buildings the resourceful *paysan* made good the damage with a patchwork of handmade brick.

BELOW: WROUGHT-IRON WORK

The iron foundries concentrated around Nontronnais bolstered the Périgourdin economy. Wrought iron, seen here on a window balcony in Beaumont, became an increasingly popular decorative material in the sixteenth and seventeenth centuries.

LEFT: LES OUTEAUX

The warm limestone of the Dordogne weathers down to pale yellows and orange, depending on the origin of the stone. The distinctive Périgourdin outeaux, a characteristic feature throughout the region, was let into the roof to ventilate the attic.

LEFT: BASTIDE TOWN

The stout houses in the medieval market place at Monpazier combine practical designs with defensive details. Wide openings at ground level sheltered the traders and their customers from the sun and rain. The bastides were originally built to settle uncultivated areas of the countryside.

Far over on the western side of Périgord, south of the spreading wheat and cattle fields of the Ribéracois, are the clay flatlands of the Double. This was a wild and desolate place where stone *croix de carrefours*, or crossroad crosses, were put up to ward off evil spirits and where the protective stonework over the village well often echoes the pine-cone shape of the *borie*. The charcoal-burners and small farmers who found no suitable building stone among the oak and chestnut forests turned to timber frame like their neighbours in the Landais. Life, however, was both hard and hazardous with stagnant marshland, buzzing with malarial mosquitoes, adding to the people's miseries. In the nineteenth century a group of Trappist monks established a monastery and farm at Echourgnac and succeeded in draining and thus reviving the land. The monastery and monks remain today, together with a few of the low, long, oak-framed buildings, the timbers filled now with brick and mortar, and the roofs clad in Roman tiles.

The two most popular regions, the chalky Périgord Blanc around the Dordogne capital, Périgueux, and Périgord Noir in the south-east, exhibit the nearest thing to a typical Périgourdin house: a steep, pixie's cap of a roof formed in flat, clay tiles runs sharply down to the last few courses, where it kicks out to form a wide, protective brim above stone walls that absorb the midday sun and glow reflectively with it, long into the evening. *Lauzes*, limestone slabs with a hole drilled to take a fixing plug of wood which was hung on the battens, were used on earlier roofs. But the cost of stone slabs, and the manpower needed to lay them, led to their being rapidly replaced when flat clay tiles became available. Occasionally the lower skirt of the roof was formed in a different tile giving the roofs an odd two-tone appearance, and the distinctive roof vents, the *lucarnes* or *outeaux*, are set like a pair of frog's eyes in the roof to keep out the rain and let in the air around the beans, onions or tobacco leaves stored below.

In eastern and northern Périgord, the front and sides of farm buildings were frequently rendered or limewashed: the *paysan* rarely worried about the appearance of the back walls since they were the least exposed to public view. But in Périgord Blanc and Périgord Noir, the wall stone, sometimes taken straight from the fields, was left bare when the cottager could find neither time nor money to cover it.

RIGHT: WREATHED IN FOLIAGE
This cottage at Trémolat, possesses a pair of outeaux *placed either side of the dormer window. Like early bricks, the small, flat, clay tiles were originally handmade and gave the buildings an individual character which mass-produced tiles were never able to emulate.*

LEFT: TRADITIONAL REVIVAL
In areas like the Double where suitable building stone was scarce, timber-framed houses were the obvious alternative. The vernacular tradition died out as mass-produced materials came into use but, as this new house near Echourgnac shows, builders are returning to the old styles and designs.

LEFT: HALF-TIMBERED TOWER
Inspired perhaps by castle watchtowers, the Périgourdin builders found towers and turrets irresistible. Since they could shelter the houseowner's pigeons, they served a practical as well as a decorative function.

The subsistence diet of the sixteenth and seventeenth centuries produced a person of considerably smaller bulk than today and the low doorway, built to fit the impoverished human frame, was sometimes the only point of embellishment. Clean columns of cut and dressed limestone, arched in earlier buildings, formed the lintel and frame and, where a render was used, the surrounds were picked out in paint.

Any further generalities about the archetypal *maison périgourdine* are inappropriate. Each community developed its own version, depending on available building materials and the social conditions of

RIGHT: COUNTRY MILL
The architectural qualities of farm buildings are sometimes ignored. Yet their sheer size suggests that more work and expense was devoted to their construction than to the farmhouse itself. This mill and granary at Saint Amand de Coly stands before a substantial farmhouse with a slate-clad, mansard roof.

RIGHT: RIVER SCENE
The River Dronne snakes through the old town of Brantôme, centred around the eighth-century Benedictine abbey and given, with some justification, the unofficial title of the Venice of Périgord.

the inhabitants. Where a settlement lay near a trade route, the householder would use any new materials that the carriers shipped in. The Dordogne river, for example, was a busy commercial waterway until the railways took away the boatmen's business in the mid-nineteenth century. Until then, builders in river ports like Domme, Lalinde and Bergerac had access to bricks and tiles as well as second-hand timbers from broken-up boats, long before the settlements of the interior.

Timber-framed buildings were more common in urban than in country settings and were especially prolific in the *bastide* towns. Constructed on as near a regular grid pattern as the terrain allowed, the

LEFT: HEARTH AND HOME
Among the maze of hipped and gabled roofs in Moulin de la Jaurie, the chimneys on one roof indicate where the farmer and his family lived.

BELOW: DOVECOT
When food was short in winter, the Périgourdin householder could always rely on a supply of fresh meat from the pigeonloft.

LEFT: PIGEONNIER
The vast dimensions of the Périgourdin dovecot near Castelnaud give this farm a church-like appearance. Both square and circular pigeonniers occur in Dordogne, the rounded form being preferred where there was little dressed stone available for the corners.

bastides were established as a means of colonizing uncultivated land and were built by the settlers themselves who each received a house, kitchen garden and plot of land in return. The newcomers were also rewarded with exemption from military service, a fact which discredits the popular supposition that *bastides* were primarily designed to serve as urban fortresses during the Hundred Years' War. The charm of *bastides* like Monpazier and Domme lies in their carefully-planned layout and their photogenic buildings: the covered market hall, the oak-framed houses, their exposed timbers sometimes protected by lines of slate, and the galleried merchants' houses.

The Périgourdin farmhouses look quite as picturesque but considerably less planned. At Sept Fonts above Périgueux a group of long, low farmhouses roofed in mellow Roman tiles seems to slide out of the hillside. A neat oval window above the door, rather than a vent in the roof, lets air into the attic, and the walls, under a pale render, are built in huge limestone blocks. At Saint-Laurent-des-Vignes in Bergerac, a more affluent *vigneron's* farm, built around a spacious courtyard with a stocky, half-timbered gatehouse at its entrance, displays a smart roof of *tuiles plates* above a *génoise* frieze.

Another farm near Ribérac is built like a church with a pigeon loft tower in the centre of the building, flanked on either side by a symmetrical roof which houses the animals on the left and the family on the right; flat tiles cover the steeper tower roof while a broad sea of Roman tiles runs down the farm and barn roofs. Even the dog-kennel by the farmhouse door is roofed with tiles.

The most basic requirements of any farming family were a fodder store, a byre and place to eat and sleep. As agriculture developed and diversified, farm buildings designed to accommodate different activities sprang up around the holding: a dry stone shed for the unfortunate geese, force-fed to make the famous Dordogne *foie gras*; the pig-sty where hams were fattened or the truffle-hunting pig was stabled; vast stone barns under a mansard roof which looked large enough to house a whole herd of cattle; and, throughout the region, the distinctive dovecot or *pigeonnier*, a square or rounded tower which occasionally housed the village bread oven at ground level.

Buildings like these are the most distinctive manmade feature in the Périgourdin landscape and, if each arrangement appears more chaotic than the last, each and every stone had its purpose and proper place in the way of things.

RIGHT: MEDITERRANEAN LOOK
This longhouse farm with a roof of Roman tiles looks as if it belongs in the south of France. One of several similar farms clustered around Sept Fonts near Périgueux, it confounds the theory that the traditional architecture of Dordogne is instantly recognizable and invariably the same.

RIGHT: SANDSTONE WALLS
One of the principal reasons for such a diversity of architecture is the rich mix of geological formations in Périgord. Clay and shale occur in the west, limestone in the centre and sandstones in the east. Equal skill went into the erection of these two walls at Villac, the one on the left in ashlar, the one on the right in neatly jointed drystone.

LEFT: PALE LIMESTONE
Walls and stone flags on the roofs of these imposing houses at Saint Genies marked the end of an era. The use of vernacular techniques for more affluent buildings gave way to new ideas and materials several hundred years before they reached the humbler farms and cottages.

RIGHT: HALLMARK OF PROSPERITY
Periods of political peace were usually marked by a surge of domestic building and the fifteenth-century economic revival, which succeeded three centuries of conflict, saw the rapid growth of towns like Beynac along the beautiful Dordogne valley.

BELOW: THE MASON'S SKILL
Decorative details, like these carvings above a door in Beynac, were more common on urban than rural buildings and were clearly the expression of a skilled craftsperson.

PAYS BASQUE

NO ONE CAN BE IN ANY DOUBT that the French have made their mark on the world. The twentieth-century concept of housing people in towering apartments has as its antecedent the seminal high-rise block of Le Corbusier's *Unité d'Habitation*, built in Marseilles during the 1950s. The materials for building these reinforced concrete monoliths owe their origins to the humble gardener, Joseph Monier, who, while working in the Versailles Orangerie in 1849, discovered a method of making flower tubs from wire coated in cement.

However, the invention of social engineering, and the materials needed to put it into practice, have been of questionable benefit. They are less a source of national pride than the contribution made by the regions to the French person's sense of national identity. Even that figure of fiction, the typical Frenchman, dressed in striped shirt, denims, beret and espadrilles, cycling down the boulevard with a string of onions on the handlebars and a baguette on the back, draws on regional differences: the shirt comes from Brittany, the denims are *de Nîmes* and the hat and shoes are borrowed from the Basques.

Unfortunately, a strong national identity and a rich regional diversity make poor bedfellows. The latter tends to be swamped by the former and brings in its wake a wave of conformity and mediocrity.

Of all the peoples who contributed to the French sense of national identity, the Basques have done so without compromising their own. They are a strange race: they have defied anthropological attempts to explain their origins; their living language, Euskara, still spoken in the high villages of the Pyrenees, is both one of the oldest European languages and quite unique; and their half-timbered houses, the woodwork picked out in bright greens, reds and blues, are like nothing else in the whole of France.

The Basque country, with its head in France and its feet in Spain, spills across the Pyrenean border in the south-west. The majority of the Basques live in the four provinces on the Spanish side, while the

LEFT: EUSKAL-HERRI
The rich diversity of French traditional buildings is brought to the fore by the unique architecture of Euskal-herri, the Pays Basque. On the French side of the Spanish frontier there are three basic types of house, each associated with its own region. This house at Ainhoa is typical of those in the Labourd region.

Aquitaine showing Dordogne and Pays Basque

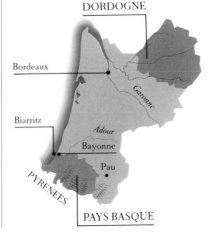

three more pastoral French regions, Labourd, Basse Navarre and Soule, collectively called the Pays Basque, are occupied by the remaining ten per cent of the people. Four and three, goes the Basque expression of solidarity, make one. The 'one' is the country they call Euskal-herri or Euskadi in Spain.

One wild theory suggests the Basques are a surviving fragment of the lost world of Atlantis. Another, pointing to the prevalence of the rare blood factor, RH negative, among Basques and distant Mayans, finds other similarities between the two cultures such as their shared passion for folk dancing and ball games. *Pelota*, once played with bare hands and a ball bound in dog skin, dominates village sports, while their high-stepping folk dances which follow complex, pagan rituals are still regularly performed.

Human evidence of the occupation of the Pyrenees goes back 40,000 years, and yet another school of thought supposes the Basque people to be the original settlers of these daunting mountains, a small and

RIGHT: HIGH PYRENEES
The natural border between France and Spain, formed by the Pyrenees, has been occupied by the Basque people for thousands of years. On sloping sites, buildings made use of the lie of the land with an entrance to the fodder store at the upper level and a ground floor entrance for the stock at the lower end of the building. A hatch inside the barn allowed the farmer to feed his animals from above.

RIGHT: ROUGH RUBBLE STONE
Despite the irregular nature of the surrounding rock, the mason managed to lay the undressed field stones in horizontal courses. Dressed stone for the doorway was impossible to find and the builder would have had to carry up some other material, like the timbers on this barn, from the valley below.

LEFT: MOUNTAIN MISTS

The climate of the westerly Pyrenees is considerably wetter than in the Alps and the functional styles of the Basque roofs were designed to keep the farmer, the stock and the fodder dry. The steep pitch and the protective half-hip over the house gable were practical measures to counter heavy rain.

hardy tribe who, when the last Ice Age drove other tribes into more hospitable areas, survived the cold on a thin diet of shellfish and snails.

When the Romans conquered the south-west corner of France, they called it the land of waters, Aquitaine. The Latin commentators, Caesar among them, recognized the Basques as a race apart from the conquered Gauls, with their discoidal tombstones carved with curious, Hindu-like swastikas and their earthy cuisine based on pimentoes, tomatoes, garlic and goosefat. The Basques continued to maintain their individuality long after the country was divided between Spain and France at the Treaty of the Pyrenees in 1659.

If anything did more to preserve the spirit and culture of the Basques it was the landscape itself, with its lowland plains, tumbling foothills and jagged Pyrenean horizon. The Pyrenees, like two of France's other natural frontiers, the Alps and the Jura, were thrust into place during the tertiary period. At the turn of the twentieth century some angry peaks still stood unconquered and as late as the 1940s several Pyrenean communities could only be reached on foot or by mule.

The political thrust for self-determination came from the industrialized Basques on the Spanish side, especially during the dark, oppressive days of the Franco regime. Then, when the secret police threatened the freedom of one of the separatists, he or she would slip across the border and hide out in the mountains, using one of the smugglers' routes that both sides regularly employed to move goods like coffee, butter and alcohol. During World War II the trade in people, refugees from either side, was brisk and lucrative, but nowadays life along the border mountain passes is quiet.

The mountain passes were well known to the Basque shepherd, the *berger*, moving his flocks of black-headed, Manech sheep, a breed renowned for their milk and wool, among the communal grazing pastures during the summer. Mountain enclosures, or *cayolars*, protected the sheep from wild animals, while the *berger* sheltered in the dry stone *cabane*, his milking churns left to drip dry outside the low wooden door. The *cabane* was protectively placed, wedged into the mountainside where the risk of a winter avalanche was minimal, or into a natural depression beside the mountain road, the hem of its slate or flagstone roof reaching down to the roadside.

On the plains, the Basque farmhouse was orientated with its back wall to the west—unlike the dry air of the Alps, the Pyrenean peaks catch and drain the Atlantic rain and the province is consequently less arid. But the Basque barns took a more defiant stance, shouldering up to what the worst of the weather could offer. The sheer size of these magnificent stone structures, which dwarf the odd single-storey cottage tucked under their leeward side, suggests that the whole community would have come together to build them. In places like the Plateau de Bénou, they possess more decorative details than the family home itself with their distinctive half-moon vents on the gable end and decorative pinnacles placed at either end of the half-hipped, flagstone or slate roofs.

The agricultural life of the Basque community has changed radically in the last fifty years. People have lost their taste for pottock, the Basque pony, once prized by the horse butcher and now more valued as a pony club mount; the area of land being cultivated, grazing stock and growing apples, maize and corn, has increased although the rural population has declined; and the new farming methods have little use for the mountainside *cabane* and lowland barn. The Basque farmhouse, however, shows no sign of becoming redundant.

These buildings made a great impression on the French architect, Eugène-Emmanuel Viollet-le-Duc, whose pronouncements had a major influence on nineteenth-century architecture. In his *Lectures on Architecture* he records:

> There is a kind of country house which architects are rarely called on to build, but which nevertheless deserves study. These districts have retained certain local traditions, which have not suffered those changes which are too often met with in many other French provinces, resulting from a passion for vulgar luxury and the desire to make a show. Silly, uninhabitable, pretentious dwellings, whose only merit is the brevity of their duration and the fact that they make simple and genuine forms seem more estimable still to persons of sense.

There are three distinctly different versions of these 'simple and genuine forms', one for each of the three French Basque regions.

BELOW: CHANGING FORTUNES
Roofs of mountain dwellings and barns might be covered with wood shingles, slate or stone slabs. The changing nature of twentieth-century agricultural life is making many of the old barns redundant, although the owner of this barn at Aucun has prolonged the life of the building with a new roof of small tuiles plates *or flat tiles.*

RIGHT: ARGELÈS-GAZOST
A house on the hillside of this Pyrenean village mirrors the simple design of the barn above, even down to the round air vent under a half-hipped gable. Elsewhere in the Pays Basque a distinctive semi-circular vent, like a half moon on its back, was used to air the roof space.

LEFT: THE SOULE HOUSE
In the low-lying areas of the Pays Basque, the three regions of Soule, Basse-Navarre and Labourd each developed their own house design. On the Soule house, like these ones near Sauveterre-de-Béarn, the clay tuile plate predominated, although the lower courses, kicked out above the eaves, were often covered in another material such as Roman tiles.

LEFT: HIGH STREET FARMS
Former farmhouses, their cart shed doors opening directly on to the street, line the road through Audaux near Navarrenx.

BELOW: NESTLING ROOFS
The tiled roofs of Soule buildings fight for space above the alleyways of Navarrenx, a bastide town still surrounded by its fortified walls.

Soule is the most easterly region, fed by the River Saison and its tributaries, filled to overflowing in spring by the meltwaters running off the Pic d'Orhy and the three great gorges of Holzarté, Kakoueta and Ehujarré. As the Saison flows north through Mauléon, the capital of Soule and manufacturing centre for the espadrille, it meanders past villages of stone and the strange, three-pointed spires, or trinity pediments, of the Soule churches. The Soule house has a tall, peaked roof which splays out at the bottom to sit on the house like an ill-fitting hat. In the west, where clay deposits were plentiful, the hipped roofs are covered in warm-red, flat tiles, but to the east, where the roofs are gabled, often with a stepped parapet at either end, slate predominates. In both cases, the householder liked to include a row of dormers well above the eaves to light the attic rooms.

In Basse Navarre, the central region of the Pays Basque, the domestic architecture is contrastingly different with the farmer's goods and chattels all gathered together under one great tiled roof. Travelling through Soule towards Basse Navarre, the houses seem to anticipate these low expansive roofs: the short splay of roof above the eaves of the Soule farmhouse begins to spread, extending out to cover a second generation of outhouses, like the dairy, wine store and cart shed, built around the original core of the house.

In the flatlands there was plenty of good building stone to be quarried but, as the hills edge up towards the Pyrenees, supplies of workable stone thin out and the housebuilder had to dredge the streams for rounded river stone, laying them herringbone fashion in the walls. The dressed stone for the corners of the building and the distinctive round arches above the door and windows had to be imported from neighbouring districts.

But stone was not always the Basques' preferred building material, for the Pyrenean foothills were once, like the rest of France, heavily forested and, until the eighteenth century, when agricultural clearance removed so much of their woodland, farms and chalets were built in good-grained oak. The evidence is still there, in the farmhouses of Labourd whose red and green painted timbers, sometimes hung with strings of pimentoes drying in the sun, gleam against their strikingly bright whitewashed façades.

RIGHT: BASSE-NAVARRE
In the central region of the Pays Basque the buildings broaden out to encompass as many of the farming activities as possible under one vast, low-pitched, tiled roof. Outside the small towns and villages, the Basse-Navarre homes of the country areas rarely display any timber work and were positioned with their backs to the prevailing westerly winds.

LEFT: DRYING PIMENTOES

Threaded on strings and hung to dry against the auberge wall, red pimentoes add an unlikely decorative touch to the Hotel Euzkadi in Espelette. The Basque language, Euskara, which gives a guttural ring to many local place names, is one of the oldest in Europe.

RIGHT: LABOURD

The maison labourd *is a huge, chalet-type building, partly built in stone and partly in half-timbered work. With up to twenty-five rooms, the farmhouse was large enough to accommodate several generations of the same family as well as a stable, workshop and dairy on the ground floor. Fodder was stored under the roof space and aired by the row of vents let in between the timbers.*

BELOW: CARVED INSCRIPTIONS

Most of the Labourd houses were originally built around an oak frame and later extended in stone during the seventeenth and eighteenth centuries. These rebuildings were often celebrated with a carefully carved inscription over a door or window lintel.

LEFT: OAK AND GRANITE
When the Labourd house was enlarged, meticulous attention was paid to the front of the buildings, with dressed granite being used around doors and windows and a finishing coat of whitewash across the façade.

ABOVE: ESPELETTE
The timber work of these vast, Labourd houses was painted in strident colours which stand out against the bright whitewash.

The first sight of the buildings in and around villages like Ainhoa, Espellette and Sare is impressive and mystifying. Bare, dressed granite blocks form abstract designs around door and window surrounds. Timbered above the ground floor, the lower storeys are built in stone, whitewashed at the front and uncovered at the back and sides. The dimensions are enormous. Nine rooms on the ground floor, ten more above and six or eight under the roof ridge were not unusual. The Euskara word for wealth, *aberat*, means a shepherd with a large flock. Surely a people who measured a man's wealth by the number of sheep he possessed could hardly afford to live in château-like dwellings of twenty-five rooms or more?

The clues to the size of the Labourd farmhouse are to be found in the inscriptions carved into the house lintels and the tombstones in the graveyards. What they record is the long lineage of Basque family names, names that go back centuries. The Labourd farm was built big enough, or extended when the need arose, to house all the members of the same family united by blood or marriage. And, rather than being inherited by the eldest male heir, the house remained in the hands of the same family for generation upon generation. Elaborate datestones, carved on the house fronts, tell the whole story.

CES TE MAISON APELEE GORRITIA AESTE RACHEPTEE PAR MARIE D GORRITI MERE D FEV JEAN D OLHAGARAY DES SOMMES PAR LVY ENVOYES DES INDES LAQVELE MAISON NE SE POVRRA VANDRE NY ENG AIGER FAITEN LAN 1662

This long inscription, running the length of a house in Ainhoa, records how the Gorritia family 'redeemed' their house with financial help from the Americas and promises that it will never again be sold or mortgaged. Several families received American aid—Columbus's *Santa Maria* was piloted by a Basque and many Basques settled the Indes as the Americas were called—and, like the Gorritia house, the datestones are centred around the seventeenth century. But Ainhoa, one of the few *bastide* towns in this area, had been established in the late twelfth century.

What the datestones mark is a period of rebuilding when, like the expanding farmhouses of Soule, an original timber-framed house was extended in stone, either colonizing the neighbouring houses on each side or, in the country, spreading out in all four directions around the central oak frame.

A typical floor plan shows stables, coachhouse, barn store, tool store, bedroom and kitchen on the ground floor, hay and maize stores and bedrooms on the first floor and further food stores in the attic. Although each family was allotted its own bedroom, one kitchen served them all and it was traditional for the men only to seat themselves at the table in the *coin à manger* to be served by the women folk. In church too, the men sat apart in their own gallery: Basque society was strongly patriarchal.

The Basques farmed the sea as well as they farmed the land although, in the case of the whalers, rather more was taken out than was put back. For centuries, fishing was a necessity and the fishermen

RIGHT: RED SANDSTONE
Local buildings were built of local stone and the town of Saint-Jean-Pied-de-Port and its neighbouring villages, which sit on a bed of red sandstone, reflect the surrounding geology.

RIGHT: SAINT-JEAN-PIED-DE-PORT
This town, built on the River Nive, mixes red sandstone with timber-framed buildings. Port *here means a mountain pass and its name refers to its position at the foot of the pass.*

RIGHT: A LOWLAND BARN

Bonding or through stones, seen here projecting from a barn wall at Verdets near Navarrenx, were used to give stability to masonry work where the stone was of poor building quality.

RIGHT: HERRING-BONE PATTERN

Down in the valleys, the builder sometimes took his stone from the river beds where the mountain meltwaters had ground the stone into manageable sizes. The pebbles made a difficult material to work with but, by laying them in diagonal or chevron patterns, the mason gave strength to the stone work and a pleasing finish to the building.

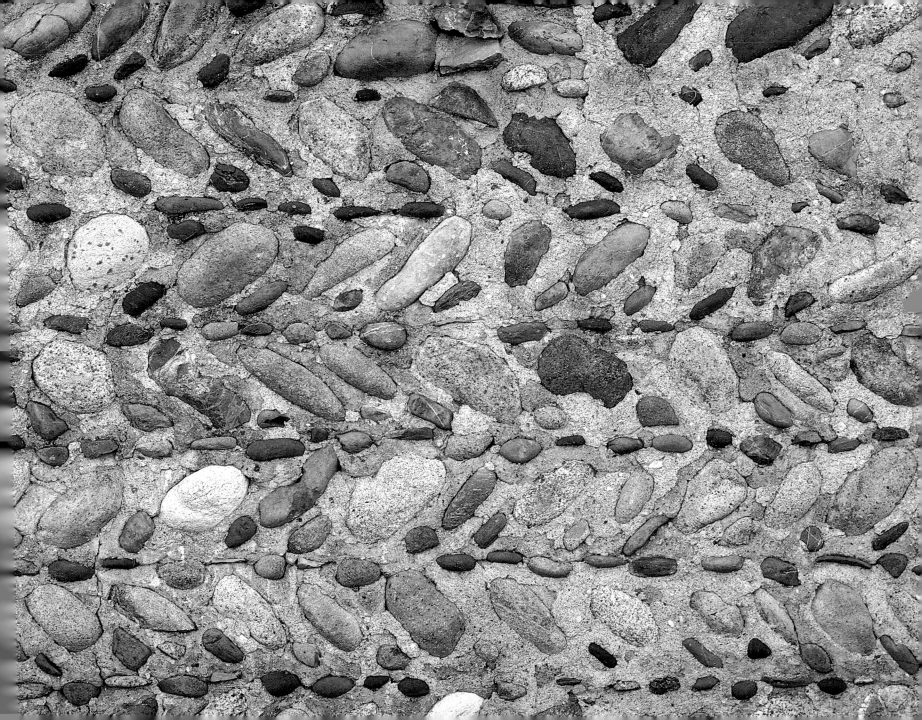

sometimes resorted to cannon and musket to defend their fisheries against the Dutch and English. The whale was an important source of food because one animal could supply the meat equivalent of fifty elephants, and whale skins went into rope-making, vertebrae into seats and ribs into house beams. Saint Jean de Luz, still the principal Basque fishing port, was once the major whaling town, but few of the traditional Basque houses here, or along the Bay of Biscay coast, survived the nineteenth-century redevelopment which put places like Biarritz on the tourists' itinerary. The best preserved examples of traditional Basque houses remain in the rural hinterland, nudged up against the Pyrenean foothills or tucked away down some lonely country road.

This is the essence of rural France. This great hexagonal country, which thrust itself so efficiently into the industrial age, has managed to retain its rural charms in quiet, out-of-the-way places. Here still are old men, comfortable in their working clothes and sustained by the local dishes, who have travelled no farther afield than the local market.

LEFT: QUAYSIDE REFLECTIONS
Bayonne, or Baiona as the Basques call it, straddles the rivers Adour and Nive. Timber frame and stone houses along the quayside reflect the traditional styles of the Pays Basque buildings.

LEFT: STREET HOUSES IN BAYONNE
Unlike the neighbouring town of Biarritz, which became a resort for the aristocracy in the nineteenth century, Bayonne remains a typical, and largely unspoilt Basque town. However, the best examples of traditional Pays Basque architecture are to be found out in the surrounding countryside.

RIGHT: HIDDEN FROM VIEW
While fastidious attention was paid to the front of the Labourd house, the back and sides, mostly hidden from public view, were considerably less elaborate. This coarse masonry is at the back of a beautiful house in Ainhoa.

BELOW: THREATENED HERITAGE
Weeds grow around the door of a derelict building in south-west France. Their remote location and the high cost of restoration means that many vernacular buildings are destined to be lost in the near future.

Quietly pickling themselves in the local brew, they curse the march of progress in a local dialect and remain grumblingly content with their homes of stone or wood, clay or brick.

True, they are a dwindling minority. In Brittany, where once they wore purple in Trégor, blue in Léon and red in Cornouaille, regional dress has become local costume, a treat for the tourist. But if the Breton *coiffe* is languishing and the patois diminishing, the regional character is still evident in the rural architecture.

However, the picturesque quality of the vernacular buildings, and the stark contrast between urban and rural life, can give rise to some rose-tinted views on the life and times of the peasant. Even the word peasant, literally a rural worker from the *pays*, has derogatory overtones which suggest that rural people are simple and ignorant.

But even the most cursory examination of the traditional buildings of rural France reveals that they were built by people with an innate understanding of natural materials, some highly sophisticated techniques for using them and a sympathetic sense of style and design. We have much to learn from them.

RIGHT: BUILT TO LAST
The traditional buildings of rural France, built to withstand the worst of the weather, have also stood the test of time. Ironically, the changing nature of the rural economy means that many have outlived their original purpose. Like the rural communities themselves, they face an uncertain future.

GLOSSARY

ASHLAR: stone cut in blocks and laid square with fine jointing.

BASTIDE: a settlement laid out on a grid plan; also a large house or farm in Provence.

BORIE: drystone shelter with a domed roof.

BYRE: cow shed.

CARRIÈRE: quarry.

COPING STONE: capping course of stonework on a wall.

CORNICE: horizontal course of stonework separating roof from walls.

DATESTONE: commemorative stone inscribed with the date of building or rebuilding.

DAUB: mud or clay.

DORMER: window pierced through a sloping roof.

EAVES: the line of the roof where it overhangs the walls.

GÉNOISE FRIEZE: decorative line of Roman tiles set under the roof eaves.

GABLE: triangular end of a building.

HIPPED ROOF: pitched roof over a gable end.

HALF-HIPPED ROOF: half-pitched roof over a gable end.

KEYSTONE: central stone of an arch.

KNEELER: the projecting finishing stone on a gable end.

MANSARD ROOF: a double-pitched roof on either side of the ridge, with the lower pitch steeper than the upper.

MAISON LABOURD: timber-framed and granite house in the Labourd district of the Pays Basque.

MAS, GRANGE: large house or farm in the South of France.

OUTSHUT: lean-to built on to the back or side of a house.

OUTEAU, LUCARNE: opening in the roof to vent the attic.

PANTILE: roof tile with a curved or S-shaped surface.

PARAPETED GABLE: low wall above the roof line, run down the gable end of the building.

PENTWIN, PENTY: Breton fisherman's or labourer's cottage.

QUOIN: stones, normally dressed, which form the external wall corners.

RANDOM RUBBLE: undressed stone laid in irregular courses.

SABOT: clog.

SHINGLES: rectangular wooden tiles used as roof or wall coverings.

THATCH: roof covering of reed, straw or heather.

THROUGHS, BONDING STONES: long stones laid through walls for extra stability.

VALLEY: sloping junction of two roofs.

VILLAGE PERCHÉ: hilltop village in Provence.

WATTLE: sticks interwoven between the framing of a half-timbered building to provide a base for the daub.

INDEX OF PLACE NAMES

Page numbers in *italics* refer to illustrations.

Ainhoa *17, 134, 149, 156*
Aquitaine 113, 139
Argelès-Gazost *141*
Armagnac 113
Aucun *140*
Audaux *143*
Auray *61*
Avallon *23, 78*

Barcelonnette *106*
Basse Navarre 136, 144, *145*
Bayonne *154, 155*
Beaumont *121*
Beine *68*
Bergerac 126
Beynac *151*
Bèze *77*
Bonnieux *111*
Bordeaux 113
Bourgeauville 40
Brantôme *112, 117*
Brittany 50–67
Burgundy 18, 68–87

Calvados 29, 30, 39
Camargue 89, *98*, 110
Camembert *48*, 49
Canal de Bourgogne *87*

Carrouges *47*
Champagne 18
Château d'Amboise 55
Château d'O *24, 45*
Collan *73*
Côte d'Or 70, 78
Cotentin Peninsula 30, 39
Côtes-du-Nord 52

Deauville *28*
Dijon 69
Domme 126, 129
Dordogne 112–133
Double 122, *124*

Echourgnac 122, *124*
Entrevaux *108*
Espelette *146, 148*
Eure 29, 39

Finistère 52, *59*
Fleys *78*
Forêt Lyons 44

Gascony 18
Gordes *93*
Grasse 89
Guerlesquin *57*
Guillaumes *109*

Hautefort *116*
Honfleur *32, 33*, 35

Île-de-France 17, 40, *79*
Île-et-Vilaine 52

Josselin 60, 62, 67
Joucas *Frontispiece*

Kervignac 67

Labourd 136, 144, *147*, 149
Lalinde 126
Landais 113, 122
Landes de Lanvaux 22
Lannion 64, 67
La Roque-Gageac 21
Les Baux *91*

Mâconnais 70, 81
Manche 29, 30
Marais Vernier *34*
Mauléon 144
Melon 55
Ménerbes *104*
Mirabeau *75*
Monpazier *120*, 129
Montignac *119*
Mont-Saint-Michel 29, *30, 31*, 39, 44
Morbihan 52
Morvan *76*, 81, 86
Moulin de la Jaurie *129*

Navarrenx *143*

Nièvre 70
Nontronnais 118
Normandy 28–49
Nuits-Saint-Georges 81

Oloron-Sainte-Marie *10*
Orbec *38*
Orne 29, 30

Paimpol *50*
Pays Basque 134–155
Pays d'Auge 30, *49*
Pays de Brays 30
Pays de Caux 30, 35, *46, 47*
Pays de Dol 67
Pays d'Ouche 30
Périgueux 122, 129
Perros-Guirec 67
Plateau de Bénou 140
Pont-Aven 56, *63*
Provence 88–111
Pyrenees 139

Quarré-les-Tombs *76*

Rhône 89, 90
Roussillon *88*
Rustrel 89

Sablat *90*
Saint Amand de Coly *126*
Saint Fargeau 74, *82, 85*

Saint Gengoux-le-National *82*
Saint Genies *150*
Saint Germain-la-Campagne *41*
Saint Jean de Luz 155
Saint-Jean-Pied-de-Port *150, 151*
Saint-Laurent-des-Vignes 129
Saint-Sauveur-sur-Tinée *107*
Saône et Loire 70
Sare 149
Sauveterre-de-Béarn 108, 109
Séguret *101, 102*
Seine-Maritime 29, 30, 35
Sept Fonts 129, *130*
Soule 136, *142*, 144

Tanlay *87*
Terrasson-le-Villedieu *118*
Thorame-Haute 110
Trégastel-plage *53*
Trémolat *123*

Vaison-la-Romaine *20*
Vaucluse 8, *92*
Vendée *10*
Verdets *152*
Versailles 18
Villac 118, *131*
Vougeot *19*

Yonne 70

ACKNOWLEDGEMENTS

I owe my thanks to Nicole Augerau, Sue Clifford and Angela King of Common Ground, Brenda Greysmith, Marie-Jo Kersebet, Annik Marsollier, Martine de Michel-Duroc, Francis Moulun, Julia Peters, M. Ribeton (Conservateur du Musée Basque, Bayonne), Simon Mole and Trevor Yorke.

Extracts in this book are taken from Edmund Blunden's poem 'Forefathers' in *The Oxford Book of Modern Verse* (Oxford University Press); Stendhal's *Le Rouge et le Noir* (*Scarlet and Black*), translated by Margaret Shaw (Penguin Classics); Pierre Lavedan's *French Architecture* (Scolar Press); and Eugène-Emmanuel Viollet-le-Duc's *Lectures on Architecture*, Vol. 2 (Dover Press).